DESIGNED to PRAY

DESIGNED to PRAY

*Creative Ways
to Engage
With God*

KELLY O'DELL STANLEY

BELONG *tour*

TYNDALE®
MOMENTUM

*An Imprint of
Tyndale House Publishers, Inc.*

Visit The BELONG Tour at www.BELONGtour.com.

Visit Tyndale online at www.tyndale.com.

Visit Tyndale Momentum online at www.tyndalemomentum.com.

Tyndale Momentum and the Tyndale Momentum logo are registered trademarks of Tyndale House Publishers, Inc. Tyndale Momentum is an imprint of Tyndale House Publishers, Inc., Carol Stream, Illinois.

Designed to Pray: Creative Ways to Engage with God

Cover designed by Kristin Bakken

Interior designed by Julie Chen

Edited by Bonne Steffen and Susan Ellingburg. Executive Editor, Leslie Nunn Reed.

ISBN 978-1-4964-0833-4

Printed in the United States of America

22	21	20	19	18	17	16
7	6	5	4	3	2	1

To those sweet friends who whisper prayers,
respond to nudges, encourage my soul, and never let go of hope—
hope that God is there, that He is listening,
and that He will show Himself in these pages.
Thank you for believing.

Surprised by Prayer

We cannot learn about prayer except by praying.
—J. OSWALD SANDERS, *SPIRITUAL LEADERSHIP*

Apparently, prayer works.

You'd think I would know that since I wrote a book about prayer. You'd expect me to live it, to never have a doubt—let alone voice one.

You'd assume that I've had a long and rich prayer life, never beleaguered by shame. Never beating myself up for not doing enough. Rarely, if ever, pulling away from God or voicing my skepticism.

Growing up, a part of me believed that you could have faith—or you could have intellect—but you couldn't have both. A "thinking" person wouldn't rely on this hocus-pocus stuff. So you can imagine my surprise when I began to embrace the Bible and try my hand at praying—not just shoot-it-up-into-the-sky prayer but sincere, heartfelt pleas. And I started to see answers.

As with many stories that become long-standing jokes, my friend Peggy and I don't remember the circumstances behind the phone call I made to her some years ago, but we both clearly remember the words I spoke in that moment: "Well, apparently, prayer works." They were spoken with exasperation and disbelief—and kind of a nagging resentment because I didn't want to become one of *those people* who held onto faith over reason. Whatever I'd been praying about, I got my answer. The situation changed. And I was left grudgingly accepting what I simultaneously wanted with all of my heart to believe: God is real.

Maybe you aren't there yet. Maybe prayer is a foreign concept to you. And God? Perhaps He's not on your radar at all. But you're curious. As you go through this book, if your curiosity turns into something more and you find yourself desiring a relationship with God, but you're not sure how to get started, you will find helpful information beginning on page 195.

I know prayer doesn't seem to make sense. I cannot prove to you that God exists or promise that you will get the answers you long for. I know it's hard to trust in something you can't see. It's easier to be cynical, to put up walls of protection, to refuse to admit that you believe. Because we're deathly afraid of being wrong.

But what if we *are* wrong?

Well, let me give you my most respectful, sincere response to that perfectly valid question: So what?

Here's the thing: I don't think you *will* be wrong. I think you will be surprised.

I'm living proof that you can be a devout believer and a cynical skeptic at the same time. At times I pose questions that appear to be an attempt to disprove prayer or faith, but my motivation is pure. I want to find God. I want Him to be everything I need Him to be, all that I hope He is. And in order to do that, I have to wrestle through the difficult questions and poke holes in my doubts.

Sir Francis Bacon wrote, "If a man will begin with certainties, he shall end in doubts; but if he will be content to begin with doubts, he shall end in certainties." In spite of my own doubts, I've seen the power of prayer. Heard it. Felt it. Witnessed it. Been transformed and blindsided and struck like lightning by it. It shouldn't work. It's too abstract and God is too big, too busy. I'm too small and incapable.

And yet I believe in it with all of my heart.

If you're one who secretly thinks that prayer is a trick of the mind, let me mention a small example to you. It's one you're holding in your hands right now—yes, this book—proof that although prayer itself is abstract, the results are often perfectly tangible.

After my first book, *Praying Upside Down*, released, I wondered about my next project. I wrote a new book proposal, even outlined twenty chapters, but it was missing an irresistible hook, so I left it simmering on the back burner. I'd been toying with a second idea, more of a memoir, and I loved the idea but felt it, too, was lacking its spark. My mind kept returning to a third idea—a prayer planner—one I'd kept mainly to myself, only describing it to a few close friends but not to anyone affiliated with my publisher.

Several months before, I had begun creating monthly prayer-prompt calendars to help people jump-start their prayers and break out of their ruts. But now I wanted to do a longer-term version, with interactive exercises, writing prompts, and room to explore and create. I enjoy helping people have fun with prayer. Pointing them toward something fresh. Hoping that along the way, they'll see a new aspect of God or grow closer to Him in ways they didn't expect.

I began jotting down some ideas here and there, and I sent up some brief prayers. *Lord, show me what to do next. How should I focus my energy? I'm stagnant right now, and I need to know what to work on. I need to write to draw closer to You, and I'm just not sure what I should be writing.*

I knew that no matter what direction God pointed me, I would keep alive the journal idea, because it had grabbed hold of me and wasn't letting go.

A week or so later, my agent, Blythe, called with exciting news. Tyndale wanted me to write a new book. It would be based on the concept of the "Prayer Palettes" from *Praying Upside Down*—sort of an interactive prayer workbook. As I read the e-mail she sent me describing the details of the concept, I found myself growing stiller and stiller.

They were describing the book I'd already envisioned.

Blythe probably wondered why I wasn't jumping for joy. My heart was beating a thousand miles a minute, but I was stunned into silence. I didn't have to evaluate the concept. I wasn't afraid I couldn't do it. I'd only spoken the desires of my heart to a handful of people, none of whom had any connection to the publishing world. And yet my publisher came to me with this book idea. The very book I'd longed to write. How do you explain that, if not for God? I didn't want to move, afraid I'd wake up and realize I'd dreamed it.

This may seem like a small, superficial thing to you. It's not life and death. It's not as critical as some needs you might be facing. It's not the biggest or hardest prayer I've ever prayed, either. But it's just one tangible example of the ways that God wows me over and over again. He surprises me, fascinates me, and baffles me, often all within the same week. It makes me want to try again, go deeper, attempt something new, ask for more, and search harder.

It reminds me that against all odds and in spite of my doubts, apparently, prayer *does* work.

HOW THIS BOOK WORKS

Which brings us back to this book, to the reason you're here. Whether you've been praying for a long time or you've never thought much about prayer, this book is designed for you.

This is an eight-week interactive workbook. Expect to spend between fifteen and thirty minutes with it each day. On the first day of each week, I will share a story with you, and then we'll fill the week with daily prayer exercises related to that theme.

You can use this book on your own or with a group. If you

use it as a group study, read Day 1 together and discuss the reflection questions as a group. Because the prayer exercises may be
private, I suggest that each person work through those on their
own. If someone wants to share her experiences during the group
discussion, welcome that, but do not pressure others to reveal
their personal prayers.

First rule: There are no rules. This book follows a consistent
structure, but *you* don't have to. It's okay if you miss a day or two.
Or if it takes you a month to finish Week 1. Feel free to cross out
my directions and write your own. Or repeat the same exercise
multiple times before moving on. If an activity doesn't interest
you, close your eyes and pray, or skip to the next page, or copy
Bible verses onto the blank pages.

Creativity is encouraged. Individuality is prized. Those things
you're afraid to say out loud? Write them in these pages. Indulge
your quirks. Find your own way. Let go of your expectations, and
trust yourself. Respond to those little nudges that point you in a
new direction.

Prayer, by my definition, is simply communication with God.
Prayer is successful when you do it. Period. This is a private place
for you to wander and stretch out your hand toward God so that
He can lead you.

DAY 1 consists of some reading, a written prayer, and a few short
reflection questions.

DAYS 2 THROUGH 6 contain a variety of interactive prayer
activities—everything from coloring pages to writing prompts to
physical objects that you can make. Some look more prayer-like
than others, but all are prayer. Each day's exercise is followed by
a mostly blank page on which you may journal, draw, take notes,
doodle—or do nothing. There's also a small prayer prompt that
you can use to keep your prayers going throughout the day.

DAY 7 closes the week with a verse or concept to meditate on, something simple and restful. This is because on the seventh day God rested—and maybe you should too (see Genesis 2:2-3; Mark 6:31; Exodus 33:14). After reading that day's entry, you can stop there—or choose to write down a prayer, journal, or use the space in your preferred creative way. The Bible tells us to pray without ceasing (1 Thessalonians 5:17)—but prayer does not have to be complicated. Simply resting in God's presence, with your mind tuned to Him, is still prayer.

In the back of the book, you'll find space to write **ongoing prayers**—the many requests you become aware of during the course of your days. There are always more needs than we can keep track of, and as you open your eyes to prayer, you'll discover so many more. Write them there and periodically go through the list praying for each one.

My hope? That you will engage with this book and give prayer a chance. Because if you are sincere about finding God in these pages, I promise you, He will let you.

Before you know it, your fears will recede, your doubts will become less important, and hope will rise up. You'll start to view God, this world, and your faith from a new perspective, one that you can carry with you for your whole life. And the prayer time that once felt stagnant or monotonous will become vibrant and exciting. You'll leave behind old prayer routines, in ordinary black and white, and surround yourself with vibrant colors and patterns. Your trust in Him will grow.

Because when you pray, you're building a relationship with God. And that is exactly what you were designed to do.

Kelly O'Dell Stanley

Facing Your Fears

*Fear is the shadow of creativity. When we choose to create,
we bring light to our fears. The darkness does not prevail
over us. The creative act is inherently an act of courage.
We are born to far too many fears and far too great a
darkness. It is only when we find the courage to create
that we are freed from those fears and that darkness.*
—ERWIN MCMANUS, THE ARTISAN SOUL

Since I started writing about prayer, I've been reminded
just how taboo the topic is. When a friend introduced me
to her friend at a luncheon and said I had written a book
the woman smiled. "Oh, that's great! What's your book
about?"

"It's called *Praying Upside Down*," I said and watched
her physically recoil. Maybe *recoil* is too strong of a word.
Still, she not only leaned back, but took a step back as
well.

Later, as this new acquaintance and I chatted over our
chicken salads, the conversation came around to the book
again, and I took the plunge. "I realize that it's ingrained
in people not to talk about politics or religion. It's hard to
talk about my book in business situations, because I don't
want people to think I'm trying to evangelize. But the
fact is, my book is about prayer, and I can't hide that."

She swallowed a drink of water as she chose her words.

"Maybe you should say 'my book is a memoir about my personal experiences with faith.' That might sound less threatening."

I've thought a lot about her words, and I've come to the conclusion that her response says more about her own experiences than it does about the way I described my writing. But this conversation reminds me how many people have been hurt by religion—people who have been pushed away from church by the ones who should have been embracing them; people who were told by others that they weren't Christians or couldn't pray the way they did; people who don't know if they're qualified to pray, if they're doing it right, if God will hear them if they're not already living 100 percent for Him.

When your experiences color your perceptions of God, you may have trouble fully embracing prayer. You might have put up walls to keep from feeling inadequate or unqualified or uncomfortable.

Can I let you in on a little secret? I feel inadequate, too.

Whenever someone refers to me as an expert on prayer, I want to laugh out loud. I *did* write a book about prayer. It's not an illogical conclusion. But if you could see inside my mind, the speed at which my thoughts spin from one topic to the next might make you dizzy.

But maybe that's the point. Perhaps that's exactly why I'm the one who wrote this. To tell you that it's okay not to be perfect. God doesn't expect perfection, and when *we* do, we're setting ourselves up for failure.

It's okay to forget to pray or to be distracted and interrupted. We can rely on the truth that God's mercies are renewed daily. To start over again tomorrow. It's all right to let God's grace carry you. It's normal to feel like you're out of your element or in over your head. It's not unusual to hold concurrent but conflicting feelings—you've been hurt by some of God's people, or seemingly by God Himself, and you're afraid. Yet you sense, somewhere in that indefinable part of you, that if you can just reach Him, it will be worth it. You are not sure, but you hope. You wonder. Whatever it is, it's *enough*.

Because there *is* one fact I know: Prayer does not get its power from me. It comes from God. From the One who hears us. Who welcomes us. Who beckons us daily, moment by moment, to turn back. To remember. To lose ourselves in Him instead of in the momentum of our overscheduled, too-full days.

The prayer activities within these pages are not a magical method for harnessing the power of the almighty God. They're simply new ways for you to reach out to Him, exercises to develop your creativity and open your eyes to discover God in a new way. Because even though God doesn't require us to vary our methods, I get bored easily—and you might too. Been there, done that, ready to try something new.

Simply by praying, simply by trying, you will meet God. You will be changed. And if you keep your eyes open in the process, you will see Him. If you listen, you will hear. You will learn to believe that He can do all the things you long for Him to do. And you'll discover that, unlike us, God never fails. He never has doubts, and He never forgets. He is the expert, the author, the authority. Our prayer is made perfect because the Perfect One receives it.

All you have to do is offer it to Him.

Won't you?

Pray with me?

God, we all come to You with certain fears. Memories of times when we didn't live up to certain standards or were misunderstood. An awareness of our failings—whether it's a short attention span, limited self-discipline, or an overcrowded calendar. Sometimes we don't know where to start or what to say. Or how to find You again after we've turned away.

But here's the miracle: You are still there. You still want to hear from us. You still care. And if we ask for help in turning to You, in finding You, You will give it.

So, we're asking. Help us. Draw our minds to You. Increase our desire for You. Let us discover that there is nothing to fear, that You alone can always be trusted. Meet us here in these pages. Make Yourself known. Amen.

REFLECTION QUESTIONS

Does fear keep you from praying?

What are you afraid of?

What made you pick up this book?

At this point, do you *believe* prayer matters—or are you here to try to figure that out?

What are your hopes?

Doodling Around

If you can't pray as you want to, pray as you can. God knows what you mean.

—Vance Havner

May I suggest that prayer has an image problem? People think it is an exclusive language reserved for holy men and women clothed in velvet robes and large hats, intoning grand words in powerful voices. Or we imagine black-clad nuns taking vows of poverty and celibacy, kneeling by candlelight in austere surroundings. We think of prayer as serious and solemn. Formal. Many pray in King James English rather than the English we use every day. *Lord, God, Thou art holy. I beseech Thee. . . .*

If that's the way you speak, more power to you. But I'm more of a slang kind of girl. I've been known to laugh while I pray. I make fun of myself. And, occasionally, I say things people think might not belong in prayer.

If I could rebrand prayer, I'd position it as approachable and rejuvenating. Informal. And yes, even fun. Approaching God with a light heart isn't irreverent. It's just being real.

So today, I want you to doodle your prayers.

DIRECTIONS: Write names or situations in the shapes already drawn on the page, and then fill in the rest of the space with curlicues and spirals, hearts and flowers, zigzags and stripes. Add more prayers. Write your name. Get out your markers and color. All you have to do to turn your doodles into prayer is to mentally offer them up to God. "As I write and draw, hear the desires of my heart and accept this as my prayer. Amen."

WRITE | DRAW | EXPLORE | PRAY

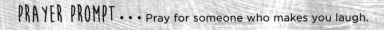

PRAYER PROMPT • • • Pray for someone who makes you laugh.

DAY
3

Rays of Gratitude

RELATED BIBLE VERSES:
Matthew 6:8; Psalm 100; Psalm 95:1-6

*Enter his gates with thanksgiving; go into his courts with
praise. Give thanks to him and praise his name.*
—PSALM 100:4

*If the only prayer you ever say in your entire
life is thank you, it will be enough.*
—MEISTER ECKHART

I don't know about you, but at any given time I could list thirty
or forty things I need. They may not all be for me—my friend
Missie needs healing, and another friend's son needs help with a
legal issue. I could stand a little more income, because money is
tight this month. And my son hurt his big toe.

There's always something.

But prayer isn't just about asking. It's also about remembering
who God is. Thanking Him for—and reminding ourselves of—
the things He has already done.

Psalm 100 is one of my favorites because it reminds us that the
best way to enter into His courts—to come into His presence—
is with praise. So today, don't ask for a thing. He already knows
the desires of your heart. Let your gratitude radiate out from your
core as you thank God for the many blessings He has provided.

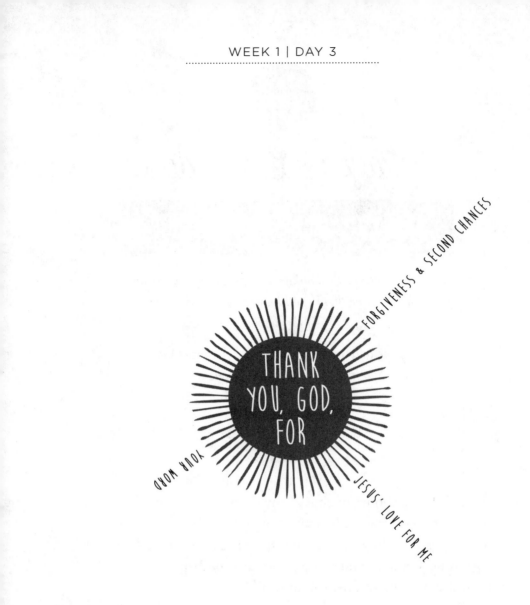

DIRECTIONS: Create individual "rays" in the accompanying sun graphic, formed by words or phrases describing something you are thankful for. And feel the warmth of living life with gratitude.

DRAW | EXPLORE | PRAY | WRITE

PRAYER PROMPT • • • Pray for someone's son.

The Posture of Prayer

RELATED BIBLE VERSES:
Romans 12:1; Hebrews 4:16

*Dear brothers and sisters, I plead with you to give your
bodies to God because of all he has done for you. Let
them be a living and holy sacrifice—the kind he will find
acceptable. This is truly the way to worship him.*

—ROMANS 12:1

I've prayed sitting in a pew. Balanced on my knees on a cushioned kneeler. Standing at the altar, hands on another person's
shoulder. In a circle at prayer group, joined hand to hand in unity.
Waiting in my car in the carpool line at school. Walking along a
beach. I've pressed my face into my carpet, distraught and word-
less, and I've stood with both arms raised high above my head
with confidence and praise.

But I've discovered that my experience changes when I alter
the physical posture of my prayer, even when my words remain
the same.

Standing with arms open toward the sky makes me feel exul-
tant. I close my eyes and imagine God's light shining upon me,
His Spirit pouring into me. I'm coming boldly before His throne.

Bowing on my knees fills me with humility. I remember who
He is and offer Him respect. I ask Him, humbly and reverently,
for help.

When I stand, arms outstretched, palms up, I'm reaching out to a Friend. In return, He grasps my hands, and we stand face-to-face, talking.

When I am facedown on the floor, awash in emotions, I am physically responding to the awesomeness of my God. I am bowing as low as I can, feeling the weight of His greatness, wanting to honor Him.

Lying in bed at night, whispering to Him, unloading the burdens I've carried all day, I feel an intimacy and can imagine His arms holding me tight as He rocks me to sleep.

DIRECTIONS: Find a comfortable spot. Close yourself in your bedroom if you want privacy. Or if you have young children, let them try this with you.

Pray in several different positions. Kneel or stand or lie down. Raise your arms to the sky or clasp them in front of you or hold your palms up on your knees. You don't need words, although you're free to use them. Focus your thoughts upward, and hold the position for a little while and see where your thoughts go.

Reflect: Pay attention to the different feelings each posture elicits. Which make you feel happier? Closer or farther from God? Awkward or comfortable? Humble and contrite or joyous and filled with praise? Journal your thoughts on the following page.

There is no right or wrong answer here . . . it's all just exploration. Reaching out to the One who wants us to encounter Him, whatever position we are in when we do.

EXPLORE | PRAY | WRITE | DRAW

PRAYER PROMPT • • • Pray for someone who has taught you something about prayer.

Stumbling Blocks

RELATED BIBLE VERSES:
Luke 7:23; Isaiah 57:14-15

It shall be said, "Build up, build up, prepare the way,
remove every obstruction from my people's way."
—ISAIAH 57:14, ESV

When I am hesitant to pray, it's often because I have a bad attitude. I'm feeling rebellious. I'm tired. In fact, there was a long time period in which I didn't pray because I was mad at God.

Some of you may be cringing, thinking, *She can't say that!*

But it's the truth. My mom died of small-cell lung cancer, and I was devastated. God—who was supposed to be a God of healing, right?—hadn't healed her. She was gone and I was alone, and I wasn't sure I could trust Him any longer. He knew what I needed—her. And yet she was no longer here.

Still I knew I should pray. I knew God would be able to bring me through it.

It just took a while before I was ready to let Him.

Maybe you don't have the stubborn, toddler-like attitude I had. But maybe you've had your own crushing pains. Maybe you were abused or someone stole your spouse or you buried a child or you're watching your parent slowly fade away.

Or maybe you see people every day who profess to be Christians but who certainly don't act like it. You don't want any part of that, so you stay away.

There are millions of reasons why we might stay away.

However, there is one compelling reason not to: God.

Only with God will we see hope again. Only through God can our brokenness be made whole, our emotions soothed, our attitudes adjusted. Only with God can we heal.

It's normal to stumble. But the best way to keep from falling is to take a close look at the obstacles before you.

DIRECTIONS: Write about the stumbling block (or blocks) that keep you from praying. Afraid God won't answer? Don't know what to say? Convinced you aren't good enough to go to Him in prayer? Whatever your stumbling block is, write it down. And ask God to remove it.

PRAY | WRITE | DRAW | EXPLORE

PRAYER PROMPT · · · Pray for someone facing a hurdle.

Faith, Not Fear

We live by faith, not by sight.
—2 CORINTHIANS 5:7, NIV

The opposite of faith isn't doubt. It's fear.

At my church, everyone prays out loud at the same time. It intimidated me at first, thinking everyone was listening, but most of the time, there's anonymity in the noise. Usually you just hear snatches of people's prayers—key words like *healing* and *hope*, *love* and *protect* jump out, but you don't hear one person specifically.

One night, though, a woman was praying for a desperate situation. Her son was being charged with attempted manslaughter. He'd dropped his baby—a horrible accident, but that's all it was. He faced jail time and the possible loss of his baby.

I'll never forget that moment. Because as I prayed for this woman, her son, and her grandson, all I could hear were her words. Three of them, repeated over and over. "Faith, not fear. Faith, not fear. Faith, not fear."

That simple act demonstrated the most beautiful kind of faith and trust. The best way to face fear is to turn in the other direction—not away from what you're afraid of, but toward what you want (and the only One who can provide it). To lean on God and trust Him even when it is scary. *Especially* when it is scary.

Every day, even in smaller things, we have a choice to make. What will you choose?

DIRECTIONS: Think about your current prayer requests. On the left side of the chart, write what it would look like to dwell on fear, and on the right, describe what it would look like to focus instead on faith. Ask God to help you with your choices and to strengthen your faith in each situation.

FEAR FEAR

FAITH

MY PRAYER REQUEST:

FEAR

FAITH

MY PRAYER REQUEST:

FEAR

FAITH

MY PRAYER REQUEST:

MY PRAYER REQUEST:

FEAR

FAITH

WRITE | DRAW | EXPLORE | PRAY

PRAYER PROMPT • • • Pray for someone in a desperate situation.

DAY
7

(DAY OF REST)

a Place of Refuge

RELATED BIBLE VERSES:
Psalm 4:8; Psalm 91; Isaiah 43:5

Do not be afraid, for I am with you.
—ISAIAH 43:5

When I was a little girl, there was a space in the cornfield by my house where the seed had washed away in the heavy spring rains and nothing grew. A small round patch of nothingness, bordered by cornstalks that were about half grown. If I squeezed between the tight rows, in just a few steps I could be in that private space, and when I knelt down, the corn surrounded me on all sides. I was only twenty or thirty feet in, but nobody outside the field could tell I was there. I felt invisible. And invincible. Because I was hiding in a safe place.

You don't need a field to find the same security.

DIRECTIONS: In your mind, go to a quiet space. Picture yourself being embraced by God. Close your eyes and simply breathe Him in. Sit in the solitude. He is with us. Not just us collectively, but with each of us, personally, individually, exactly the way we need Him to be. Right now. And when we are with Him, we are in the safest of all possible places. Whether anyone can see us or not. Thank Him by coloring in the next page.

DRAW | EXPLORE | PRAY | WRITE

PRAYER PROMPT • • • Pray for someone's safety
(emotional, physical, or any other kind of security).

DAY 1

Letter to My Fourteen-Year-Old Self

The LORD is like a father to his children, tender
and compassionate to those who fear him.
—PSALM 103:13

Dear sweet girl,

You lie there in the angle of light bent around the door, in that sheltered, private spot where the light illuminates your papers, but your parents, in the living room downstairs, can't see you from where they are reclining. The white-painted posts from the stairs in the hallway outside your door cast striped, curvy shadows across the carpet, and you hear the faint noise of a laugh track from the television below. You can't see her, but you know your mom is wrapped in a soft blanket, quietly turning the pages of a book until she yields to her yawns and goes to bed.

In that sheltered place, you make charts on graph paper, carefully checking off each prayer as you pray it daily and transferring your prayer list to a new sheet of paper when you've filled every box. Maybe your prayers aren't prompted by passion. You've never seen that before and don't know to aspire to it. You're not sure what your mom would think of you praying, but you're certain that it's wrong to be up past bedtime.

At the same time, you're strangely determined to master this prayer thing. To do it right. You feel your way through. But you're on your own. This isn't a lifestyle you've witnessed yet. Your eyes slide down the list, praying lofty wishes—that God will heal the sick and handicapped. That He will help you stop all your bad habits and become a better person. That He will forgive you of all your sins and help you follow all the rules.

You don't know yet that *religion* is not what you want. What you want is *Him*. But all you know are the words you've heard a handful of people say, so you mimic them, offering big, general, dutiful prayers.

You pray the same words, night after night. Over time, they will lose their meaning.

One day prayer itself will lose its meaning.

You'll run out of words when your mother is no longer downstairs—or anywhere on this earth—because you aren't entirely sure who you are without her. As a teen, you haven't experienced God speaking to you personally yet—but later, when you stop hearing Him, you'll feel the loss deep in your gut. As an adult, you'll stare at the occasional lines printed in red ink in your Bible and fight an internal war. A part of you has always believed, has always yearned for the balm that those words might bring. Something drew you to these words long before you knew why, but eventually the time will come when you begrudge every spark of hope you felt reading God's promises because now you know that there isn't always a happy ending.

Thirty-some years from now—when the house you grew up in has been sold, and your dad has moved south to a warm climate and a new relationship, and Mom's Lands' End bathrobe has been donated to Goodwill and her contact deleted from your phone—you'll ache at the memory of the young girl who was so sheltered and naive.

You're no longer tiptoeing around the shadowy edges of your room, avoiding the squeaky floorboards. Now you're tiptoeing around the edges of your faith. Wanting God, but not wanting to be caught wanting Him. Wanting to hold tight to promises that sometimes seem to be false.

But yet? You'll marvel at the fact that God saw fit to plant those tender shoots of faith in the stripes of light falling across your bright blue carpet. That in the silence between the creaking floorboards, He whispered into your soul a desire for words that you wouldn't need for many more years. The funny thing is, through all the changes over those three decades, one thing never changed.

What you need now is what you needed then. And it's not a cute boy. A flirty look. Or straight *As* on your report card.

You feel a bit of desperation, wanting to exist in that world again, the one where the worst thing that can happen is that you'll be caught out of bed at 11:00 p.m. You want to go back to wherever it is that Mom yawns in her bathrobe and prayers can be mastered with nothing more than graph paper and colored inks.

But sweet girl? That sheltered place? It still exists. It doesn't reside in the house your family no longer owns. It's not to be found only in a church. Because even if you don't always like the words you hear, God still whispers. He still holds you close.

And you'll find that even in the midst of pain, God's presence is the only balm. When you hurt enough that you'll finally fumble through the words to ask God to fill your soul, to smooth over the gaping wounds of loss and disappointment and loneliness— well, that's when He will pick you up in His arms and hold you in the shelter of His heart.

And you'll know that you were never alone. That you were

never abandoned. That when you face the crippling sorrow, when you let God back in to feel it with you, you'll find something new. Reminiscent of the past, and not always easy, but in some ways better.

Because along the way, you'll discover that you're safe in your Father's arms, and that you've found your way home.

Pray with me?

Father God, wrap Your arms around me. Hold me safe. Let me understand deep in my core that I am Your child. That I am safe and sheltered and protected by You. Surround me with an awareness of Your unconditional love and Your never-ending presence. And let me not overcomplicate this but come to You with simple, pure, unshakable faith. Amen.

REFLECTION QUESTIONS

Describe the place in the world where you feel most safe.

Do you associate safety and security with God?

Consider other times and places in your life where you have felt safe. What aspects of these moments do you want the shelter of God to provide?

How did your childhood beliefs affect your beliefs as an adult? What enhanced or hindered your spiritual journey?

Back to the Beginning

Over time, we become so familiar with verses or repetitive poems that they lose their meaning. Today, we're going to go back. And try to remember.

DIRECTIONS: Choose one of the following children's prayers or songs (or add your own). Copy it into the frame on page 31 in colored pencil, crayon, or marker; then get down on your knees or assume another prayerful posture and pray it sincerely and with meaning.

Thank you for the world so sweet.
Thank you for the food we eat.
Thank you for the birds that sing.
Thank you, God, for everything.

Now I lay me down to sleep.
I pray the Lord my soul to keep.
Keep me safe all through the night,
and wake me with the morning's light.

God is great, and God is good.
Let us thank Him for our food.
By His hands we all are fed.
Give us, Lord, our daily bread.

Jesus loves me—this I know,
For the Bible tells me so,
Little ones to Him belong,
They are weak but He is strong.

Jesus loves the little children,
All the children of the world.
Red and yellow, black and white,
All are precious in His sight,
Jesus loves the little children
  of the world.

EXPLORE | PRAY | WRITE | DRAW

Filling in the Blanks

As down in the sunless retreats of the Ocean,
  Sweet flowers are springing no mortal can see,
So, deep in my soul the still prayer of devotion,
  Unheard by the world, rises silent to Thee,
    My GOD! silent, to Thee—
    Pure, warm, silent, to Thee.

—THOMAS MOORE, "AS DOWN IN THE SUNLESS RETREATS"

𝓘'll admit it. Sometimes it's hard to pray because I don't know what to say. Often it's not that there is something big or that I'm overwhelmed. I'm just tired. Or I don't feel very passionate. I'm bored or uninspired. It's not always big things that keep us from coming to God. It can be the little things, too.

Ways around this include talking to Him anyway—and trusting that words will come. Or adopting someone else's words as your prayer (songs, psalms, liturgy, poetry). Or simply filling in the blanks in the following activity.

DIRECTIONS: Read Psalm 116 in its original form on the left for direction, but let yourself be creative as you fill in the blanks on the right in "your" Psalm 116. Write whatever comes to mind—whatever you see, think, feel, or have experienced.

PSALM 116

¹ I love the LORD because he hears my voice
    and my prayer for mercy.
² Because he bends down to listen,
    I will pray as long as I have breath!
³ Death wrapped its ropes around me;
    the terrors of the grave overtook me.
    I saw only trouble and sorrow.
⁴ Then I called on the name of the LORD:
    "Please, LORD, save me!"
⁵ How kind the LORD is! How good he is!
    So merciful, this God of ours!
⁶ The LORD protects those of childlike faith;
    I was facing death, and he saved me.
⁷ Let my soul be at rest again,
    for the LORD has been good to me.
⁸ He has saved me from death,
    my eyes from tears,
    my feet from stumbling.
⁹ And so I walk in the LORD's presence
    as I live here on earth!
¹⁰ I believed in you, so I said,
    "I am deeply troubled, LORD."
¹¹ In my anxiety I cried out to you,
    "These people are all liars!"
¹² What can I offer the LORD
    for all he has done for me?
¹³ I will lift up the cup of salvation
    and praise the LORD's name for saving me.
¹⁴ I will keep my promises to the LORD
    in the presence of all his people.
¹⁵ The LORD cares deeply
    when his loved ones die.
¹⁶ O LORD, I am your servant;
    yes, I am your servant, born into your household;
    you have freed me from my chains.
¹⁷ I will offer you a sacrifice of thanksgiving
    and call on the name of the LORD.
¹⁸ I will fulfill my vows to the LORD
    in the presence of all his people—
¹⁹ in the house of the LORD
    in the heart of Jerusalem.

Praise the LORD!

MY PSALM 116

¹ I love the LORD because _____

² Because he _____

     I will _____!

³ _____ wrapped its ropes around me;

     the terrors of _____ overtook me.

     I saw only _____ and _____ .

⁴ Then I called on the name of the LORD:

     "Please, LORD, _____ me!"

⁵ How _____ the LORD is! How _____ he is!

     So _____ , this God of ours!

⁶ The LORD protects those _____ ;

     I was facing _____ , and he saved me.

⁷ Let my soul be at rest again,

     for the LORD has been good to me.

⁸ He has saved me from _____ ,

     my _____ from _____ ,

     my _____ from _____ .

⁹ And so I _____

     as I live here on earth!

¹⁰ I believed in you, so I said,

     "_____ , LORD."

¹¹ In my _____ I cried out to you,

     "_____ !"

¹² What can I offer the LORD for all he has done for me?

¹³ I _____

     and praise the LORD's name for _____ .

¹⁴ I will keep my promises to the LORD

     in the presence of all his people.

¹⁵ The LORD cares deeply

     when _____ .

¹⁶ O LORD, I am your servant;

     yes, I am your servant, born into your household;

     you have freed me from my chains.

¹⁷ I will offer you _____

     and call on the name of the LORD.

¹⁸ I will fulfill my vows to the LORD

     in the presence of all his people—

¹⁹ in the house of the LORD

     in the heart of Jerusalem.

Praise the LORD!

PRAY | WRITE | DRAW | EXPLORE

PRAYER PROMPT • • • Pray for someone who is a protector (your spouse,
a pastor, a law enforcement officer, a soldier, a mother or father).

The Fingerprints of God

RELATED BIBLE VERSES:
Isaiah 49:16; Psalm 31:15

Powerful is your arm! Strong is your hand!
Your right hand is lifted high in glorious strength.
—PSALM 89:13

If you've watched NCIS or CSI or any of those other initial-laden television crime shows, you know that every person has unique fingerprints. The specialists always have to run them through a database to identify them. In other words, until the results appear, they don't know whom the fingerprints belong to.

We're going to work backwards—since God always does the unexpected, since Jesus always turned the world's expectations upside down. We're going to start by knowing who we're looking for (God), and then we're going to identify examples of where we've found His fingerprints in our lives. Because God's hands are big enough and strong enough to hold all that we need. You can count on it.

DIRECTIONS: Start by asking God to show you who He is, what He has done for you, and where you have seen Him. Then write down five things you want to remember about God next to the thumb and fingers on the handprint below. Many believe that in the Bible the number five symbolizes God's grace. As you read over what you've written, remind yourself that these are your personal representations of God's grace and goodness, foundational truths you can lean on when you're afraid or uneasy or worried.

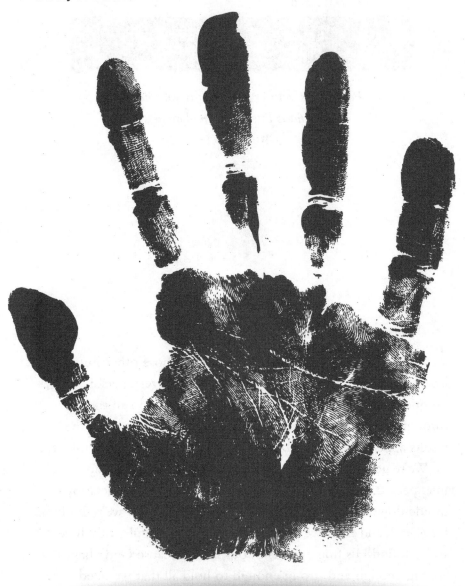

WRITE | DRAW | EXPLORE | PRAY

PRAYER PROMPT • • • Pray for someone whose hand you've held.

Daddy, Is This Okay for Me?

RELATED BIBLE VERSE:
Romans 8:28

*Trust in the LORD with all your heart; do not depend
on your own understanding. Seek his will in all you
do, and he will show you which path to take.*
—PROVERBS 3:5-6

*M*y son, Bobby, was diagnosed with severe food allergies when
he was eleven months old. His dad and I taught him that he
could not eat or drink anything without checking with us first.
One day when he was four or five, he ran to me, out of breath,
holding a snack his class was about to share. "Is this Bobby-okay?"
he panted. When I said yes, he smiled and ran back out to eat it.

That day I realized something. Just as Bobby could not
consume one thing without asking if it was okay for him, we, too,
should bring every desire to God. Even the small stuff. And once
He says yes, we can fully embrace what He offers.

DIRECTIONS: Imagine you're a young child asking your heavenly Father
for what you want. Draw a picture of you holding it out to God (or simply
draw a picture of what you want). Then, just as if you were in school, use
your best penmanship to write out your request. Be straightforward and
direct. Then pray, *God, this is what I want. Is it okay for me?*

DRAW | EXPLORE | PRAY | WRITE

Alphabet Prayers

*"I am the Alpha and the Omega—the beginning and
the end," says the Lord God. "I am the one who is, who always
was, and who is still to come—the Almighty One."*
—Revelation 1:8

*K*ids love blocks. So do adults. Whether we're spelling words
with alphabet blocks or building towers, we all have fun with
them. The letters in the alphabet are the basic building blocks of
our language. They can also be the building blocks of your prayer,
an elementary way to get started. It's a simple process, but not one
without power. God called Himself the Alpha and Omega, the
beginning and ending letters of the Greek language, showing that
He encompassed everything—every bit of language, every utter-
ance of our words.

DIRECTIONS: Ask God to call to mind certain people or problems you can pray about; then under each letter, write a word or phrase starting with that letter. As you write the names and situations, pray about each. Alternatively, you could fill in the blanks with people and things for which you are grateful.

EXPLORE | PRAY | WRITE | DRAW

PRAYER PROMPT . . . Pray for someone who uses the alphabet in a direct way on a daily basis—a teacher, journalist, writer, speech pathologist, interpreter.

DAY
7

(DAY OF REST)

A Father's Love

RELATED BIBLE VERSES:
Romans 8:15; 1 Corinthians 8:6;
Matthew 23:9; Romans 8:38-39

*If you took the love of all the best mothers and fathers who
have lived in the course of human history, all their goodness,
kindness, patience, fidelity, wisdom, tenderness, strength, and love
and united all those qualities in a single person, that person's
love would only be a faint shadow of the furious love and mercy
in the heart of God the Father addressed to you and me.*
—BRENNAN MANNING, *THE FURIOUS LONGING OF GOD*

DIRECTIONS: As you color in the verse on the adjacent page, soak in
this truth: God loves you more than you can imagine. Dwell in this place
of awareness. Allow yourself to be overcome with gratitude for the God
whose love is so strong and glorious, for the Father who loves you with
a fullness you can only begin to comprehend. Let yourself feel small and
vulnerable, and know that Daddy is in control.

Reflect: What has getting to know God taught you about being a parent
(whether you are one or not)?

PRAY | WRITE | DRAW | EXPLORE

PRAYER PROMPT • • • Pray for parents who are divorced but have a child together.

Making Connections

The creative person wants to be a know-it-all. He wants to know about all kinds of things—ancient history, nineteenth century mathematics, current manufacturing techniques, hog futures. Because he never knows when these ideas might come together to form a new idea. It may happen six minutes later or six months, or six years. But he has faith that it will happen.

—Carl Ally

One afternoon, in an attempt to avoid the work deadlines I was facing, I did what anyone would do and took an online personality quiz. I don't remember what it was about—what 70s song best describes you, or what color is your dominant emotion, or some other thing—but I remember a question that temporarily stumped me.

What is your strongest skill?

I'd like to say my hesitation was caused by the plethora of abilities I have to narrow down, but sadly that was not the reason. The first thing that came to mind was "making connections between things," and I hesitated because I wasn't sure how to say that or what it even meant. Was it a valid answer?

Apparently, yes, because two days later I happened upon a definition of creativity: making connections between unrelated things.

That's what I do, both as a graphic designer and

writer—notice patterns, find what's similar, look for the common denominators.

One of the first—and only—rules of brainstorming is to not discredit an idea right off the bat. It's important not to limit your thinking up front. As you begin to evaluate your ideas later, you may find various reasons they might not hold up or be appropriate in a given situation. But when brainstorming, you have to let go of your fear of being wrong and give all your ideas a chance.

Thomas Edison invented the lightbulb (among other things), but the process wasn't without its hurdles. In fact, when talking about trying to perfect the lightbulb, he is quoted as saying, "I have not failed. I've just found 10,000 ways that won't work." Until he knew that one approach did not work, he gave it consideration.

In prayer, you cannot fail—unless you simply don't try. The success of prayer isn't measured by how many yes answers God gives you. I confess, there are times I have used prayer as a way to direct the will of God, not accept it. I've tried to tell Him how to answer and what to do. And then God has given me the grace to recognize that His way is better than mine. Not just once or twice, but always. Sometimes I discover that what I want happens to line up with what He wants, but not usually.

Prayer's benefit is not about any kind of measurement, but rather it's about the process—learning, seeing, listening, changing. It's about relationship—growing closer, learning to depend more on God. It's about power—realizing that you cannot carry it all, change it all, or handle it all on your own, but acknowledging that God can. And He will. If you'll ask.

I've seen all kinds of creative answers to prayer—proof to me that God's creativity far surpasses my own. My husband, Tim, was let go from his job about eighteen months ago (as I write this). On New Year's Eve, as he was closing the auto shop he managed, his supervisor informed him he didn't need to come back. I'm self-employed and had a business trip in New York the following week, and Tim was planning to come spend a couple of days with me after my work was done. Well, at least this meant he didn't have to use his vacation days.

While we were there, the Midwest was hit by a blizzard, and our flight home was cancelled. We were stranded in New York City. It's not cheap to get last-minute hotel rooms, or to eat, or to do much of anything there. But we had a really, really good trip despite spending money we thought we might need later.

When we got home, my work level exploded. I could only do it all if all I did was work—which I did. Because Tim was home, he was able to run our kids to practices, take food to them before games and meets, throw in a load of laundry, and run to the grocery store to make our dinners. Because I had the capacity to work more, I earned more—enough to pay the monthly COBRA health insurance premiums while Tim looked for a new job. Five months later, he found one, right about the time my work slowed back down.

I've prayed for help managing excessive workloads and had clients decide they were no longer in need of the services my fellow contractors and I supplied. I've prayed for help with our finances and had unexpected refunds and payments suddenly arrive.

You needn't worry if you don't think you're creative. God is, and He will provide the creative solutions. All you have to do is be willing to try. We are created in His image, and the ways in which we embrace our creative natures will help us to become more like Him.

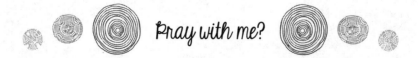 *Pray with me?*

Dear Lord, sometimes it's a little intimidating to try something new. But I hold tight to the truth I've discovered as I've walked this path with You: As long as You are in it, I want to be there too.

Change can be painful at times, and sometimes I fight it. But Your vision surpasses mine, so I surrender myself willingly. When You get involved, when You begin to refine me and smooth the rough edges, I don't become less but more. Open my heart and mind to new possibilities, and teach me to express my creativity in ways that allow me to find You. Make connections for me between people and ideas and my awareness of You—let me see more of the ways You've woven us all together and connected us all with Your love. Amen.

REFLECTION QUESTIONS

Do you think of yourself as creative? Why or why not?

Have you noticed answers to prayer that seemed unexpected? What happened?

Did you realize they were God's answers at the time or only in hindsight?

DAY
2

Jumbled-Up Words

RELATED BIBLE VERSES:
1 Samuel 16:7; Romans 8:26

Moses pleaded with the LORD, "O Lord, I'm not very good with words. I never have been, and I'm not now, even though you have spoken to me. I get tongue-tied, and my words get tangled."

—EXODUS 4:10

Some days we can't find words when we pray, and other days there are so many that they get all jumbled up and discombobulated. That's not all bad, though. Are you familiar with Magnetic Poetry, the magnetic word tiles people use to create sentences or phrases on their fridges?

Try that today with prayer. You can ask for things, thank God for what He has already done, or praise Him for who He is. Maybe a new prayer will jump out at you. Or maybe this will make no sense at all. But exploration in prayer is meaningful. God knows your heart. This is really just for you. Mix it up. Enjoy.

DIRECTIONS: Create your own words to cut apart, or download a list I have created at **kellyostanley.com/word-tile-download/**. Shuffle the individual words, and start arranging them into sentences or phrases. If you'd like, record some of your favorite combinations below.

SAMPLE:

CREATE YOUR SENTENCES HERE:

WRITE | DRAW | EXPLORE | PRAY

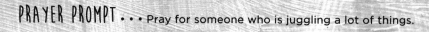

PRAYER PROMPT • • • Pray for someone who is juggling a lot of things.

DAY
3

Prayer Mapping

Creativity is just connecting things.
—Steve Jobs

I took a humanities course during my freshman year of college. As much as I now love to read and write, discussing classic literature right after lunchtime made me especially sleepy—warm classroom, full tummy, and the lack of sleep caused by the near all-nighters I pulled regularly as an architecture major.

But one day the lesson woke me up because my professor was describing stream of consciousness. Developed by a group of writers in the early twentieth century, it was meant to express the flow of thoughts and feelings in a character's mind. It relates to the way one thought triggers another and then another, and before you know it, you're in a whole new place. I thought, *Finally! That's what you call the way I think!*

If "stream of consciousness" sounds too fancy, think about "Six Degrees of Kevin Bacon." It's a game based on the concept of six degrees of separation, which supposes that any two people on earth are six or fewer acquaintance links apart. In this game, people challenge each other to find the shortest path between an arbitrary actor and Kevin Bacon.

You can put this thought process—the concept of making connections and seeing how interrelated we all are—to work in your prayers. Because we're all connected, one way or another.

DIRECTIONS: Write the name of someone important to you in the center of the page. Who or what is connected to that person? His or her children? Businesses? Relatives? Spouse? Draw lines from the original name, connecting them to others. Thoughts of one child might make you think of someone else's child. Draw lines between them. Praying for one friend's marriage may remind you of another couple who needs prayer. Diagram the trajectory of your prayers, noticing the parallels and intersections. Go to **kellyostanley.com/prayer-mapping** to see a sample.

DRAW | EXPLORE | PRAY | WRITE

PRAYER PROMPT ... Pray for God to strengthen
your connections to others.

The Many Names of God

Who is God except the LORD? Who but our God is a solid rock?
God is my strong fortress, and he makes my way perfect. He makes me as
surefooted as a deer, enabling me to stand on mountain heights.
—2 SAMUEL 22:32-34

Over the years, I've noticed multiple sides to my husband. There's the childlike, fun-loving side—sort of like the character played by Tom Hanks in *Big*. There's the serious, strict side, which my kids see from time to time. There's the vulnerable side (he may or may not need tissues to watch *The Land Before Time*). There's the strong side (he can open any jar of pickles, carry big bags of water-softener salt to the basement, and kill spiders). There's the spiritual side (there's nothing like seeing your man pray with your children). There's the tender side (he still constantly tells me I'm beautiful—and means it—even after twenty-five years of marriage). And there's the generous side (anything he has, including his time and expertise, he will offer to you if he knows you need it). Certain aspects are more noticeable at different points in time, but all of them come together to make him who he is.

The Bible includes many different names of God. When I try to fathom the full picture—all the aspects that each name represents—it makes my brain hurt because I'm just not equipped for such magnitude. And yet, just as I've experienced with Tim, I understand that my love for God is more full when I am aware that He's multifaceted. He is the sum total of all of His names, simultaneously, through and through.

DIRECTIONS: Read and reflect on the meaning of the following names for God, and then think through your prayer list. Match each person to the facet of God that most meets his or her needs and write the person's name on the line. Mention the facet of God as you pray for him or her.

ABBA

God our Father,
our dearest Daddy
(Romans 8:15)
Praying for _____ .

EL-SHADDAI

The Almighty,
All-Sufficient God
(Genesis 17:1; Revelation 1:8)
Praying for _____ .

JEHOVAH JIREH

The Provider
(Genesis 22:14)
Praying for _____ .

JEHOVAH SHALOM

The God of Peace
(Psalm 29:11)
Praying for _____ .

JEHOVAH ROPHI

The Lord our Physician
(Psalm 103:3)
Praying for _____ .

JEHOVAH ROHI

The Lord, my Shepherd
(Psalm 23:1)
Praying for _____ :

MELEKH HAGOYIM

King of the nations
(Jeremiah 10:7)
Praying for _____ .

EXPLORE | PRAY | WRITE | DRAW

PRAYER PROMPT • • • Pray for someone who has the same name as you.

DAY
5

Color Palette of Prayer

RELATED BIBLE VERSES:
Genesis 9:13-17; Ezekiel 1:28;
Revelation 4:3; Revelation 10:1

Colors speak all languages.
—JOSEPH ADDISON

The rainbow symbolized God's promise made to Noah in the book of Genesis, at the beginning of the Bible—and is seen again at the other end, in the book of Revelation, when the glow that encircles God's throne is like a rainbow.

In other words, these colors represent His promises—made visible.

Colors often portray specific concepts. Green relates to money. Red often suggests an emergency. Blue calls to mind a tranquil waterscape or vast sky—safety and stability. Purple indicates royalty. Yellow represents sunshine and happiness while orange makes us think of fire. Connect the colors of your choice to each of your needs.

DIRECTIONS: Select a color for each heading—Healing, Provision, Deeper Faith, Freedom (from temptation, from crisis, from addiction), Peace, Forgiveness—a color to represent each need listed. Then, in the open spaces on the grid, write the names of every person and set of circumstances you can think of. Use your color palette to fill in the spaces with the color representing the types of prayers you're offering for that person.

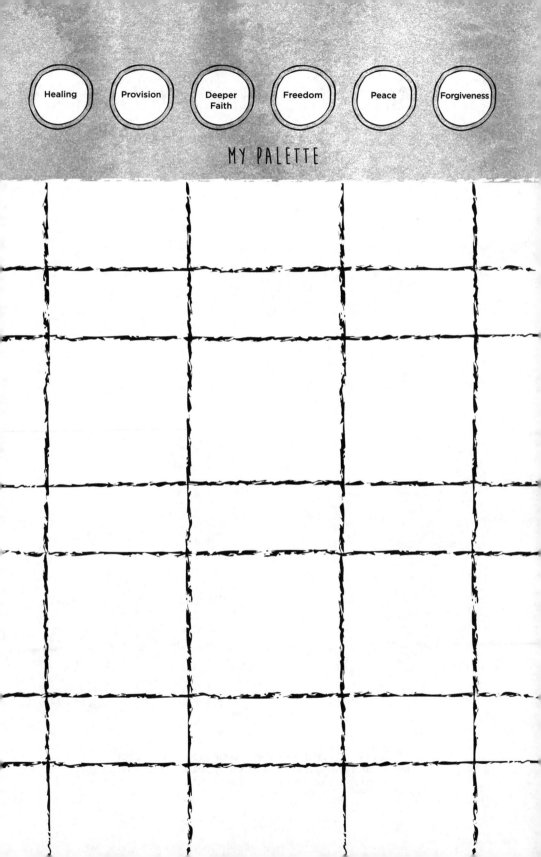

Healing   Provision   Deeper Faith   Freedom   Peace   Forgiveness

MY PALETTE

PRAY | WRITE | DRAW | EXPLORE

PRAYER PROMPT • • • Close your eyes and let your finger land somewhere within the graphic you created. Pray for that person or situation throughout the day.

64

More than One Way to See Him

Every truth has two sides; it is as well to look at both,
before we commit ourselves to either.

—AESOP

We often miss the answers to our prayers because we assume the answer will look a certain way. But God's answers are often radically different from what we expect. Depending on the perspective we choose, a situation can be seen in many different lights.

Recently, my father-in-law passed away quite suddenly. He had cancer, but what killed him was a separate infection that quickly ravaged his immunocompromised body. The whole family has been heartbroken.

But here's the thing. We can view his loss as a tragedy and wallow in despair, believing God didn't hear our prayers. Or we can recognize that he was spared the extreme pain from the cancer he had. On the day he passed away, we learned there were no registered bone marrow donors in the world who were compatible, and without a match, doctors could not cure him. He didn't suffer a prolonged fight but went peacefully and quickly, surrounded by family and cushioned by prayer.

In the following illustrations, notice that the pattern is the same and so are the colors. But because of the arrangement of the colors and the ways they are concentrated, the two designs look remarkably different.

DIRECTIONS: As you color the designs on these pages, create various patterns. Consider using mostly light colors on one set of shapes and dark on the other, or lots of green in one and mostly purple in the other. Visually create a larger shape—see how different you can make it. Or design it to look like stained glass, with transparent colors that overlap. Where you place the colors determines what shapes emerge and which recede.

While you're coloring, think about a time when you felt as though God didn't answer you (or didn't answer in the way you wanted Him to). Ask Him to help you see another perspective. If you look for the beauty in a situation, you will find it.

WRITE | DRAW | EXPLORE | PRAY

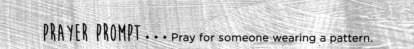

PRAYER PROMPT • • • Pray for someone wearing a pattern.

DAY
7

(DAY OF REST)

Bringing Prayer to Life

RELATED BIBLE VERSES:
Micah 6:8; Matthew 25:40

Faith does not live in our heads. It lives in our
hearts and in the work of our hands.

—MARK LIEBENOW

God filled the Bible with spiritual truths—guidance and instruction, promises and hope. Many of us focus on our personal faith, which is important. Even Jesus went off by Himself to pray.
But after He had done so, He got up and went about His day. And along the way He loved people—by truly seeing them. By helping them. By teaching them. And by serving them.

Our culture has changed the word *love* into an emotion, but in biblical times, the word denoted action. It was a verb. Simply thinking about our feelings is not what God had in mind. We're cheating ourselves and ignoring a critical part of living the life Jesus makes available to us if we're not doing things for others. It's time to get moving.

I know this is your "day of rest," but consider taking a short walk and think about opportunities to put yourself and your needs aside for someone else's benefit. Picture the people in your life and ponder practical ways to help them. Match their needs to your abilities and abundance. Or match your passion to a known need. Don't limit your thinking to only "spiritual" things. Service is about helping others. It's about building relationships, letting people know that they are loved and welcomed and that they are not alone.

For example, invite a single mom over for dinner. Or mow your neighbor's yard. Can you pick up groceries for someone recovering from surgery? Do you have some spare cash to hand to the man standing with a sign near the street corner? Is there a shelter where you've always thought about volunteering (or a clinic or a food pantry or a library)?

Because when you offer yourself that way (your time, abilities, or money), you are bringing Jesus to others. Whatever you do selflessly for others, you do for God.

We're only focusing one day on this, but don't let this be the end of it. As prayer transforms the way you look at the world around you, you may find yourself wanting to do more for others in response. You may find yourself reaching out more and more, expressing your faith in your actions. Before you start moving forward, let's pray together:

Dear Lord, it makes me uncomfortable to reach out to strangers—and sometimes even to friends. I worry what they will think. But I am realizing that serving others touches me and them in a profound way. We both benefit. Guide me in the right direction. Help me to let go of my fears and embrace the opportunity to connect with others through You. Let this be just the beginning of a lifetime in which I step back and let You take the lead. Use me to help Your light shine into other people's lives. Amen.

DRAW | EXPLORE | PRAY | WRITE

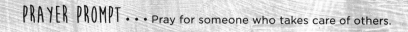

PRAYER PROMPT • • • Pray for someone who takes care of others.

Carrying the Mat

RELATED BIBLE VERSES:
Luke 5:18-20; Proverbs 27:17; Proverbs 18:24;
1 Thessalonians 5:11

*Some men came carrying a paralyzed man on a sleeping mat.
They tried to take him inside to Jesus, but they couldn't reach
him because of the crowd. So they went up to the roof and
took off some tiles. Then they lowered the sick man on his mat
down into the crowd, right in front of Jesus. Seeing their faith,
Jesus said to the man, "Young man, your sins are forgiven."*
—LUKE 5:18-20

*M*y dad had just been diagnosed with cancer. Stupid,
stinkin', blasted cancer. I'd lost my mom to that awful
disease nearly three years earlier. Believe me, I didn't want
my dad to have to go through this. I'll be honest, I didn't
want to either.

And that's when my friend Sandee stepped in, just like
the friends of the paralyzed man. She knew what I was
struggling with and came beside me one day and prayed.
In that moment, I laid down the worries I had and let
her words wash over me. When she finished, she put her
arm around me and squeezed, saying, "I don't want you to
have to go through this again."

When Sandee prayed, I pictured the men carrying their
helpless friend on a mat to Jesus. Feeling the urgency, they
changed their plans on the spot and headed up to the roof

when they couldn't get through the crowd in the house where Jesus was. Tearing off mud and tile, making lots of noise and a big ol' mess—everyone surely noticed what was going on, but no one stopped them. By the time the men carefully lowered their friend down to Jesus, their muscles were straining, sweat dripping.

It didn't matter, though, because they knew what Jesus could do for their friend. And they knew their friend couldn't do it for himself.

I went home and read all three accounts of this story in the Bible (Matthew 9, Mark 2, and Luke 5). Nowhere does it say that the paralytic *asked* his friends to take him to Jesus. That's what I'd always assumed. It makes sense to me that the one in need of healing would need to take the first steps (literally or figuratively) toward the Healer.

But in this case, I think it was his friends. They took it upon themselves to carry him. To put him where he could receive help—help that they couldn't give him. And when they finished their mission, Jesus said to their friend, "Young man, your sins are forgiven." And then He healed the man's body, too. As always, the soul was healed first. As always, Jesus knew just what was needed.

The paralyzed man's friends carried him to Jesus. And Sandee carried me to Jesus in prayer.

Having friends like this can help—literally and figuratively—to carry us through. I'm fortunate to have many of them.

My friend Peggy is remarkable. She's fun—always up for whatever you have in mind. She's generous and thoughtful, a passionate and capable leader who works hard. She loves high-heeled shoes, Twizzlers, and chocolate chip cookies. She delights in children and makes every person, young or old, feel like they are the one and only person she wants to see at that moment.

God is everything to her. First and foremost, with passion and intensity and joy and intention. When we're together, she'll ask tough questions and speak the hard things to me in love. She'll press me to recognize when I'm deluding myself. She keeps my secrets and knows just when to make fun of me and when to stop.

The very best thing about Peggy is that she prays for me when I ask. And even when I don't. I know that whatever I'm doing, her prayers are helping to guide me, cushion me, protect me, and inspire me.

The Bible talks about a "friend who sticks closer than a brother" (Proverbs 18:24, NIV). And 1 Thessalonians 5:11 says "Encourage each other and build each other up, just as you are already doing."

Sometimes being a good friend means showing up un-announced with donuts and lots of time to listen. Other times, it might mean skipping the donuts (but still listening). But the one thing we can *always* do—pray—matters. It's the utmost expression of love. When we can't fix a problem ourselves, we know who can. And even if He doesn't fix it the way we hope, we know that our friends are always better off simply from stepping into His presence. As are we.

So next time you see a friend struggling, don't wait for her to ask for help. Lift up a corner of the mat, and carry her to God. Sure, she might be able to do it herself, but it's also possible that her body—or faith—may be weak. Your friend may feel fright-ened, alone, filled with shame, or overwhelmed with the sheer magnitude of the problem. Perhaps she's lost direction, or maybe she isn't even aware of what she truly needs.

But Jesus tells us to pray about everything, and to pray for one another. Every one of us needs prayer. All the time. In the process of praying, you'll find that God will change you. He will soften your heart, show you how to forgive past wrongs, extend second chances, and help you to love the ones you're praying for, whether they believe in God and prayer or not. If *you* believe, that's enough. If you're not sure, but you're giving God the benefit of the doubt, that's enough, too. If you don't really think it will help, but you're out of options, prayer is still a valid action to take. The very act of reaching out in prayer is motivated by hope—hope that God is real, hope that He will hear, hope that He can help.

And hope lightens even the heaviest hearts.

Pray with me?

Precious Lord, what a privilege You've given us by asking us to pray. You don't need our help, but You want us to draw near to You, whether we walk there under our own power or are carried by our friends. Give us the desire to grab hold of our friends' mats. Give us the strength to help carry the weights that burden us. Help us reach out in this form of love every day, grabbing hold of a different mat to help carry another, until we've laid the whole world at Your feet. Amen.

REFLECTION QUESTIONS

Has a friend ever helped carry one of your worries or concerns? Did it help?

People often say that when you share your struggles with someone else, somehow the emotional weight feels lighter. Why do you think that is?

Who in your life right now can you help carry to God? What needs can you place before Him for someone you love? List them below.

Untangled

We learn the rope of life by untying its knots.

—JEAN TOOMER

$\mathcal{T}$hink of your problems as tangles or knots. I don't know about you, but I'm pretty impatient when it comes to untangling things. When my necklaces get twisted together or a drawstring gets tangled in the laundry, I go to my husband, exasperated, after an agonizing (and eternal-seeming) ten seconds of trying to fix it myself. I'm more likely to tug pieces apart (breaking something in the process) than I am to have the patience to figure it out myself. Lucky for me, my husband has that kind of patience.

Lucky for us, God does too.

DIRECTIONS: Grab a hole punch and a piece of string at least a yard long. (If you don't have string, use a piece of ribbon from your giftwrapping supplies or an old shoestring.) Create your own tags from a piece of thick paper, such as card stock or index cards. Punch a hole near one end of each tag. Write prayer requests onto the tags, and thread the string through the holes. Tie a knot. A few inches down the string, add another tag, and then another.

Pause at each knot to pray. As prayers are answered, you can pull off the paper tags—and, if you want, untie the knots as a visual reminder of what God has untangled. You can also partner with a friend and swap your string of prayer requests with hers, praying for her needs through the week, one knot at a time.

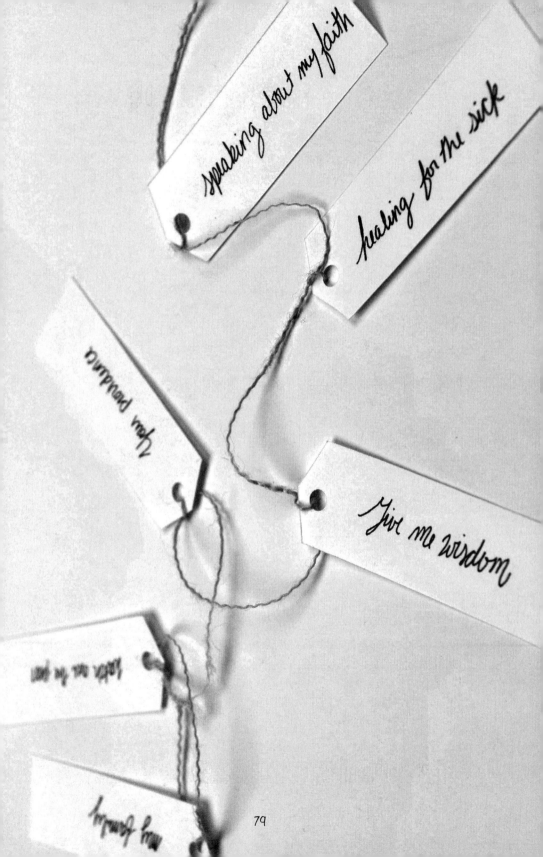

79

EXPLORE | PRAY | WRITE | DRAW

PRAYER PROMPT ••• Pray for someone you've prayed *with*.

Prayer Symbols

The soul . . . may have many symbols with which it reaches toward God.
—ANYA SETON

*O*ur society is built on symbols—simple representations of a specific concept. We've trained our minds to translate any combination of colons, semicolons, dashes, and brackets into a face that is smiling, frowning, winking, or otherwise. We've also learned to recognize certain logo symbols, which often connote more than the object they depict. Emotions, desires, feelings. For instance, Target's logo conjures—for me—feelings of happiness: a chance to meander the aisles, appreciating good design, color, patterns. Overflowing shopping carts. An escape from my regular routine. The logo no longer simply represents a retail establishment but a whole experience.

(And suddenly, I'm feeling the need to head to the nearest Target. But I'll resist. For now.)

Several years ago, my friend Lisa taught me about assigning objects to represent different people in my life and using those objects as visual reminders to pray. Lisa's husband, Mike, is a big John Wayne fan, so whenever she sees an image of John Wayne— on TV, on a DVD case in a store, in a magazine—she prays for Mike. As I mentioned earlier, my friend Peggy (who is Lisa's friend too) loves chocolate chip cookies. When Lisa sees chocolate chip cookies, she says a prayer for Peggy (and then enjoys one in Peggy's honor).

Most of us probably already connect certain objects with a friend, child, spouse, or parent. Using these symbols as prayer markers is just taking those passing impressions to the next level—elevating them from a fleeting thought to a God-bound prayer. The idea is to choose something that reminds you of the person you want to pray for, something you're likely to see or hear during the week. You can choose a sound (a teakettle whistling or a specific song), a person (real, fictional, or cartoon), a color (the choices are endless), or an object (a Harley, a commuter train, a certain tree or flower). You can pray for each of your family members as you fold their laundry.

DIRECTIONS: In the following chart, list important people in your life along the left-hand side. In the center column, brainstorm words and concepts that you connect to those people, and then in the third column, write (or draw) your final selection. As you go through your days, watch for these symbols—and pray.

IMPORTANT PEOPLE	WORDS/CONCEPTS I CONNECT WITH THEM	FINAL WORD/SYMBOL I CONNECT WITH THEM

PRAY | WRITE | DRAW | EXPLORE

PRAYER PROMPT . . . Pray for a business (small and local or meganational corporation) whose logo you like (or one you don't).

Forwarded Message

RELATED BIBLE VERSE:
James 5:16

To be a Christian without prayer is no more possible than to be alive without breathing.

—MARTIN LUTHER

You know that, right? It's why so many of us assure others, "I'll be praying for you."

If you're anything like me, you mean well. Every time. But in practice? Well, maybe we're not always so great at following through. Our minds move on to the next thing and *whoosh*, there go our good intentions, right out the window. Along with so many other things.

So here's a tip: When you say it, stop and pray. Right then.

It's a divine privilege to pray for someone else. When you pray for someone with a sincere heart, God opens within you a new understanding, deeper compassion or empathy, and stronger love for that person. To intercede, or pray on someone else's behalf, is to let God connect you deeply to that person through prayer. To weave a seamless, ethereal fabric of His love across space and time.

DIRECTIONS: Ask God to open your heart and show you whom you can pray for today. There's no formula for this—just talk to God, but do it in writing. After you've written it in the circle, snap a picture to send by text or e-mail, or copy it onto a notecard to mail. You don't need to give a lengthy explanation about why you're sending it. Just say something like "You're on my mind today, and this is what I'm praying for you." And then pray. Let them see this evidence of your love for them. It's a beautiful gift that only you can give.

WRITE | DRAW | EXPLORE | PRAY

PRAYER PROMPT • • • Pray for the last person who sent you a text or e-mail.

Family Tree

Blessed are those who trust in the LORD and have made the
LORD their hope and confidence. They are like trees planted along
a riverbank, with roots that reach deep into the water. Such trees
are not bothered by the heat or worried by long months of drought.
Their leaves stay green, and they never stop producing fruit.

—JEREMIAH 17:7-8

When I lost Mom four years ago to cancer, I expected to be sad. What I didn't expect was the way that, without her, I felt uprooted. Without the force of her personality or her daily physical presence, I wandered aimlessly, trying to figure out who I was. Until that time, I didn't know how strongly rooted I was in my identity as her daughter.

And yet, as the veil of grief lifted and I was able to see those who were still here with me, I realized what a strong support network I had. Family, yes, but also friends. Mentors. Fellow moms. Friends of my parents. Acquaintances who reached out to me with encouragement. Cards and e-mails and texts, telling me how much Mom meant to other people. And what I discovered is that my "family" extends way beyond those who share genes with me. I've been shaped by the influence of a variety of people and grounded by their love.

It's a beautiful family tree, unshakable—because even when one root withers or a branch falls away, the rest of the tree remains strong.

DIRECTIONS: Inside the roots, write the names of family members (or others who are like family) who have influenced your life and are dear to you. As you write each name, offer up a brief prayer for that person, and don't forget to give thanks for those who helped establish the roots of your faith.

DRAW | EXPLORE | PRAY | WRITE

PRAYER PROMPT • • • Pray for someone who has helped
someone else's faith take root (not your own).

Gallery of Influences

RELATED BIBLE VERSES:
1 Peter 5:1-5; 1 Timothy 4:12

Blessed is the influence of one true, loving human soul on another.
—GEORGE ELIOT

If you ever invite me over, don't be offended if I don't seem to be listening to anything you say. I'm probably busy looking at all of your framed photos, the artwork on the walls, which books are on your shelves. I love observing what matters to someone and trying to figure out why.

Chances are good that if someone's picture is in a frame, it's someone you love. We only frame photos of people who matter. But in reality, the people who have made a difference in our lives have not all been people we love. We're also influenced by people who have hurt us, criticized us, or brought out aspects of our personality or behaviors we're not particularly proud of. All of our experiences and relationships, whether positive or negative, shape us profoundly.

DIRECTIONS: Scroll through the gallery of your mind, jotting down names (or drawing portraits) in each frame. Color them if you wish. As you think about each person, lift him or her up in prayer. Give thanks, ask forgiveness, pray for healing—or go with whatever comes to mind.

INSPIRED ME

BEFRIENDED ME

FORGAVE ME

ENCOURAGED ME

SHAPED MY BELIEFS

BROUGHT OUT MY BEST

TAUGHT ME

WAS THERE FOR ME

EXPLORE | PRAY | WRITE | DRAW

PRAYER PROMPT • • • Pray for someone who
has invited you into his or her home.

(DAY OF REST)

When the Holy Spirit Prays

RELATED BIBLE VERSES:
John 17:9; John 17:20; Romans 8:26-30

The Holy Spirit helps us in our weakness. For example, we don't know what God wants us to pray for. But the Holy Spirit prays for us with groanings that cannot be expressed in words.
—ROMANS 8:26

Perhaps the best part of writing books about prayer is witnessing the way God uses prayer to encourage me. Every time I start to flounder in my writing, I get a message from someone saying, "I'm praying for you." Often that is followed by words that address my exact struggle, proving to me that God is personal and active and that prayer makes a difference. (Yes, even after all this time, I still need that proof once in a while.)

Even when I don't get that, though, God is praying for me. The Bible promises that we don't have to know what to pray for because the Holy Spirit does. The Holy Spirit is the third person of the Trinity—God the Father, God the Son, and God the Holy Spirit—who is also known as the Helper. He guides us, teaches us, and prays on our behalf. We don't need to know the right words; all we have to do is spend time in prayer and let God do His thing.

You've spent the week praying for other people. So today, sit back and let Someone else pray for you.

DIRECTIONS: Read the related Bible verses on the previous page and then go to God. Expectantly. Trust that God knows what you need and that He will pray even when you can't. Color in the verse below.

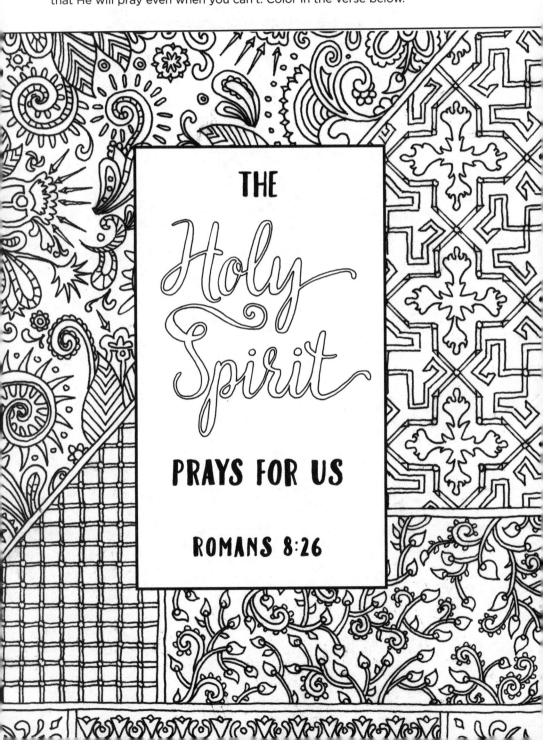

THE *Holy Spirit* PRAYS FOR US

ROMANS 8:26

PRAY | WRITE | DRAW | EXPLORE

PRAYER PROMPT • • • Pray for the first friend you remember
having and for the most recent friend you've made.

Personally Designed

RELATED BIBLE VERSES:
Romans 12:6-8; Esther 4:14

The creative is the place where no one else has ever been.
You have to leave the city of your comfort and go into
the wilderness of your intuition. What you'll discover
will be wonderful. What you'll discover is yourself.

—ALAN ALDA

I have one younger sister, Kerry. Our dad, who loves us completely and totally and with an unconditional love, has a standing joke when we call: "Is this the pretty one or the smart one?" After all these years, it still makes me laugh, and depending on how I feel that day, I give him a different answer. We both know he thinks both of us are pretty and smart. My dad has found a way to always let us know we're special to him. If you would ask Kerry, she'd claim she's his favorite. I, of course, know better. (Because I'm pretty *and* smart.)

One night, when my friend Sandee and I were talking, she said, "Don't you ever, sometimes, imagine that you are God's favorite—just for that moment?" At the time, I couldn't say that I did. I wasn't important enough. I didn't know Him well enough. The only thing I knew was that I was jealous. I didn't even know I wanted that special distinction until I heard her talk about it.

And yet, in spite of my actual qualifications, God looks at me and says, "Is this the pretty one or the smart one? The faithful one or the prodigal? The one who's with Me all the time or the one who just found her way back?" And *whatever* the answer, it doesn't matter. He already knows. He holds out His arms in welcome and says, "You, My child, are My favorite."

How can that be? It makes no sense to us, particularly as women who are conditioned to compare ourselves to others (usually finding ourselves lacking in the ways we measure up). We're too fat, too short, too insecure. We've become conditioned to expecting the reward to be commensurate with our abilities. If we're talented, we will succeed. If we're pretty, we will find a man.

It's a short step to apply that concept to "if we're faithful, God will like us."

God wants us to be more like Him, but He takes us just as we are—and multiplies what we have into something more. I love color and words and design. To me, there's nothing more exciting than hearing people's stories about God, but I'm an introvert. So God has filled my life with clients who have become friends and provided opportunities to talk about Him. He's used my love of design and writing to allow me to tell people about Him without having to stand in front of crowds on a stage. Of course, He's given me opportunities to do *that*, too, because He sees potential even when we do not.

Romans 12:6-8 says, "In his grace, God has given us different gifts for doing certain things well. So if God has given you the ability to prophesy, speak out with as much faith as God has given you. If your gift is serving others, serve them well. If you are a teacher, teach well. If your gift is to encourage others, be encouraging. If it is giving, give generously. If God has given you leadership ability, take the responsibility seriously. And if you have a gift for showing kindness to others, do it gladly."

See? He doesn't want to make you into something you're not.

He wants to make you into the most-fully-you possible. Don't shy away from that. Figure out what you're good at, what you love, what you need, and embrace it.

It is only when we fully express ourselves, pouring it all out for Him, that we become fully alive. When we operate from that place, God becomes visible. Removes obstacles. Relieves fears. Opens doors.

And shows Himself to be more than we ever hoped.

Pray with me?

Master Designer, help me to stop resisting change. Show me how to embrace myself—just the way You made me. Let me look for You in the midst of my talents and abilities, my failings and strengths. Let me see You in Your wholeness as I search to find myself in the fullness of You. Let me believe that, for just this moment, I am Your favorite. Let me live in that knowledge, and let it fuel me to always want more. Help me to use that passion to deepen my faith, to increase my desire to know You better. Amen.

REFLECTION QUESTIONS

Do you believe you are special to God? Why or why not?

What abilities, talents, and passions did God give you?

What practical steps can you take to develop them more fully or put them to greater use?

What worries, fears, or obstacles keep you from using your gifts more?

Get Real

*The LORD doesn't see things the way you see them. People judge
by outward appearance, but the LORD looks at the heart.*
—1 SAMUEL 16:7

You've seen them on Facebook or Instagram—the people
with the ideal lives. You've rolled your eyes at the status updates
from the perfect family with the adorable kids (or if you haven't,
I sure have)—everyone color-coordinated, all of them excelling
at sports, academics, and friendships. Not to mention the healthy,
visually stunning fresh meals, shiny new cars, and clever hashtag
commentary.

With the advent of social media, our society has embraced the
idea of only showing our best. Granted, some show their very
worst—but for the most part, people want to make themselves
look beautiful, successful, and popular. There are several inherent
problems: One is that others cannot relate to you in your perfection. It sparks jealousy and feelings of I-can't-live-up. Another is
that it's hard to keep pretending. Eventually the facade will fall
and people will see your real self.

But remember: God knows the truth, whether you tell Him
or not.

I've had great breakthroughs in my prayer experience when
I've quit pretending and gotten real with God. When I approach
Him with my defenses down, He has shown me new truths about
myself and about Him.

Ready to give it a shot?

DIRECTIONS: Write a Facebook status about your biggest struggle, the least ideal or most problematic thing in your life. Be specific, not vague, and be honest about what's really happening. (This isn't going to be seen publicly.) What do you think will happen? What's the worst-case scenario? Do you truly believe it will all be okay?

Now write a new status update, as though God is writing about your problem, either giving advice, offering you insights or hope, or simply looking at the situation from a greater distance (with an eternal perspective). Don't limit God, and give Him the benefit of the doubt that He is able to do this.

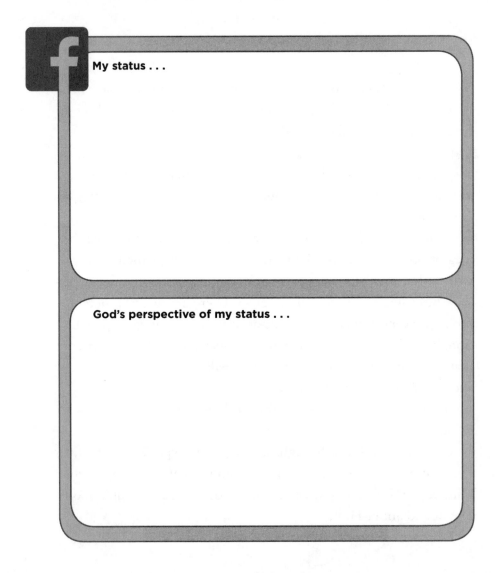

My status . . .

God's perspective of my status . . .

WRITE | DRAW | EXPLORE | PRAY

PRAYER PROMPT · · · Pray for the friend whose status
update on Facebook appears at the very top of the page.
(If you're not on Facebook, try Twitter, Instagram, or Pinterest.
Or select a name at random from your phone contacts.)

Losing Your Baggage

RELATED BIBLE VERSES:
Matthew 11:28-30; Isaiah 53:4

Jesus said, "Come to me, all of you who are weary and carry heavy burdens, and I will give you rest. Take my yoke upon you. Let me teach you, because I am humble and gentle at heart, and you will find rest for your souls. For my yoke is easy to bear, and the burden I give you is light."
—MATTHEW 11:28-30

Jesus promised that His yoke is easy to bear, His burden light.

A yoke is a wooden frame that harnesses two animals—usually oxen—together side by side. It allows them to share the weight they're carrying. When Jesus refers to this "yoke," He's talking about the burden of following and fulfilling all the dos and don'ts of the religious leaders. In contrast, following Jesus is easy and light.

Sometimes it doesn't feel that easy. Oh, it may be simple enough to *say* we believe. And yet there are days when we're bogged down by the weight of our worries.

Do you carry around guilt? Do you think you're not qualified to talk to God? That He doesn't want to listen because of that thing you did? Or the one you didn't do that you should have? Do you think you can't pray since you don't go to church? Maybe you're bogged down by the *I-shoulds* (I should volunteer more, give more, care more) and *I-shouldn'ts* (yell at my kids, hold a grudge forever).

Maybe you're loaded down with pain or shame. Desperation—for God to save the life of someone you love, for the money to come through, for the marriage to work out. Or are you angry because your parent, spouse, or child died? Because your best friend betrayed you? Because your son can't overcome his addiction?

What is it that you would like to run away from? What baggage do you drag around, making it hard to forget or let go?

DIRECTIONS: Pack away your burdens, large or small, inside these suitcases. You may draw them or jot down words. Whatever you carry that slows you down, that cripples you, hand it to God to carry. For each weight, ponder its importance and then repeat after me:

Lord, it's too much for me. I'm tired of carrying it. I give it to You. I trust that You will help me, that You will lift the weight of this, because I wasn't designed to carry this. I don't want to take it back once it's in Your capable hands. Amen.

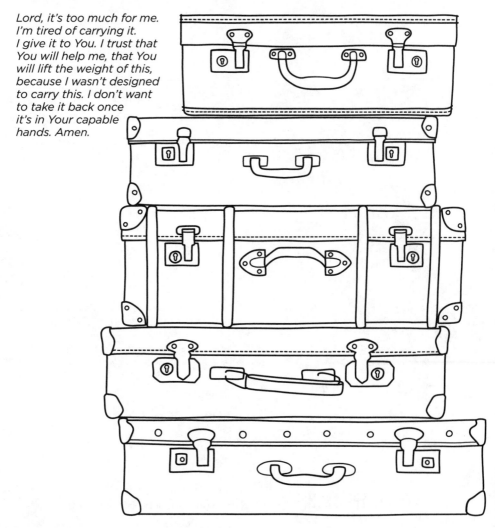

DRAW | EXPLORE | PRAY | WRITE

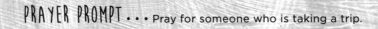

DAY 4

Snapshots of God

RELATED BIBLE VERSES:
Hebrews 13:8; Malachi 3:6

We now see that to know Christ is to love him. It is impossible to have a vision of his face, to behold his person, or understand his offices, without feeling our souls warmed towards him.
—CHARLES SPURGEON, *THE SAINT AND HIS SAVIOUR*

God may not always let us in on what He's doing, but He *has* let us in on who He is.

In Week 3, we looked at a few of the names of God mentioned in the Bible, but there are more characteristics to Him than we can name. He doesn't change—He is and always has been all that He is. But as *we* have new experiences, our perceptions of Him change.

When I was twelve, I imagined God as a kindly grandfather in the clouds. At twenty-three I pictured Him as formal, severe, and powerful. Holding my newborn daughter, I was in awe of the Creator of such an intricate, delicate thing. Many years later, I could envision Him walking beside me, reaching out His hands, smiling and talking, as approachable and real as a friend.

Accepting that one of these faces of God is true does not cancel out another. God exists outside of space and time, so the facet you saw at a given moment does not define or encompass Him. He is not one or the other; He is all in all.

DIRECTIONS: Reflect on the turning points in your life and what you believed, saw, knew, learned, or felt about God. Include moments like your baptism, giving birth, getting married, losing a parent—or otherwise ordinary moments in which your awareness of God changed. Within the center of the photo frames, sketch these pivotal scenes or write about the aspect of God you experienced at that moment in time. If possible, write the approximate date of the memory along the edge of the photos.

After you finish, close your eyes and imagine the God you know right now. The sum total of all the individual moments you just drew. Write a prayer of thanks to Him for being all that He is.

EXPLORE | PRAY | WRITE | DRAW

PRAYER PROMPT ... Pray for someone who was present during one of your turning-point moments.

Suiting Up in Armor

RELATED BIBLE VERSES:
Ephesians 6:10-18; Isaiah 59:17;
Romans 13:12; Ephesians 4:24

Put on your new nature, created to be like God—truly righteous and holy.
—EPHESIANS 4:24

I doubt you've ever dropped the word *breastplate* into a daily conversation. It's a little weird to think of today, but it describes exactly what this piece of armor was: a plate of metal fashioned into a sleeveless "shirt" that covered the upper chest and torso—protecting the vital organs of the wearer.

"St. Patrick's Breastplate," a poem based on words attributed to St. Patrick in the fifth century, contains these beautiful lines:

> *Christ be with me, Christ be within me,*
> *Christ behind me, Christ before me,*
> *Christ beside me, Christ to win me,*
> *Christ to comfort me and restore me.*
> *Christ beneath me, Christ above me,*
> *Christ in quiet, Christ in danger,*
> *Christ in hearts of all that love me,*
> *Christ in mouth of friend and stranger.*

I imagine if St. Patrick had a set of armor, these words would have made a nice engraving, identifying who was always at his side. The Bible tells us in Ephesians 6:13-17 to put on all of God's armor. This armor is for protection, a means of defense, not attack. This includes the belt of truth, the breastplate of righteousness, the shoes of the preparation of the gospel of peace, the shield of faith, the helmet of salvation, and the sword of the Spirit. In other words, we should wrap ourselves in the traits and goodness of God, relying on His strength and trusting in His protection.

St. Patrick's poem memorably portrays a fundamental truth about God—He is present and available to us everywhere at all times. That gave the Irish saint comfort and strength. What gives *you* confidence and peace?

DIRECTIONS: As you ask God to cover you with His goodness and righteousness, decorate your own pieces of armor. Use symbols that represent what you are counting on—peace, hope, light, healing, the Holy Spirit— or that connect to one or more aspects of God (Father, King, Alpha and Omega). While you draw, thank God for all the ways He has protected you.

PRAY | WRITE | DRAW | EXPLORE

PRAYER PROMPT • • • Pray for someone whose "feet carry the gospel" (a pastor, someone married to a pastor, a missionary, or a small group leader).

DAY
6

What God Sees in the Mirror

RELATED BIBLE VERSES:
Genesis 1:27; Genesis 16:13; Isaiah 43:1

You are the God who sees me.
—GENESIS 16:13

I have called you by name; you are mine.
—ISAIAH 43:1

*A*s women, so many of us struggle with insecurity. We're either *too much* in some ways or *not enough* in others. Even if we have people in our lives who love us and affirm our worth, at some point we may have been made to feel inferior or shameful, worthless or insufficient. It's difficult to banish these thoughts once they've found their way inside our heads.

But God loves us. He sees us, He knows us, and He claims us. There *must* be value in us.

Take a look in the mirror and, just for this moment, suspend judgment. You might be surprised by the beauty you see.

DIRECTIONS: Ask God what He sees when He looks at you. Find a large mirror and as you look at your reflection, write or draw on the mirror with a dry erase marker (or even lipstick), focusing on seeing yourself as God might. For example, outline your lips on the mirror and write "speaks encouragement" or "friendly smile." You might draw around your hand and write "gives willingly" or "takes care of family." Add some of your self-discoveries to the mirror below.

WRITE | DRAW | EXPLORE | PRAY

PRAYER PROMPT ••• Pray for a teen or anyone
else you know who is insecure.

DAY
7

(DAY OF REST)

Inscribed on His Hand

RELATED BIBLE VERSES:
Isaiah 49

Since we can't literally see God, it can be difficult to believe that we—individually, personally—matter to Him. The Bible is full of people begging God to show them that He was there, that He remembered them. When Isaiah declared that Israel—God's chosen people—had been hidden in the shadow of the hand of the Lord, God responded that He would never forget Israel and would always protect them. As proof, He said, "See, I have written your name on the palms of my hands" (Isaiah 49:16).

DIRECTIONS: Accept this promise for yourself today as you doodle your name all over this hand. What does it mean to you to place your life into His almighty hands?

SEE, I HAVE WRITTEN

YOUR NAME

ON THE PALMS OF MY HANDS.

ISAIAH 49:16

DRAW | EXPLORE | PRAY | WRITE

PRAYER PROMPT • • • Pray for someone you've forgotten about (search the archives of your mind for old friends, classmates, or coworkers).

Making Some Changes

RELATED BIBLE VERSES:
Psalm 18:2; 2 Samuel 22:3; Psalm 91:4; Psalm 17:8

*Faith today is not enough for tomorrow. It must
be constantly renewed by a conscious act.*

—LUCI SHAW

My mom was sarcastic and cynical and funny, even when
she didn't mean to be. One year, as my husband and I
celebrated another wedding anniversary, she remarked, "As
much as you like change, it's a miracle you and Tim are
still together." About the multiple layers of paint colors in
the various rooms in my house, she said, "If you measured
these rooms, they're probably a foot smaller than they
were when you moved in."

In other words, I like change. I get bored easily. My
mind rarely stops (or even slows down). I have a million
things I should be doing at any point in time. More ideas
than time to implement them. New clothes every season,
not because I have lots of disposable income but because
I'm ready for new patterns and colors and styles.

More prayer requests than I could ever remember. Lots
of faith in God.

And yet—some days, I'll confess, the thought of sitting down on the couch in my living room to still my mind and focus my thoughts on things above makes me groan.

Don't get me wrong. I don't mean it as a rejection of God. Not at all. Just a rejection of the same ol'-same ol'.

The Bible tells us that God never changes. He is the rock underneath our feet. The wings that shelter us. The steady, almighty, perfect God.

But *we* change, don't we? Sometimes for better, sometimes for worse.

In my marriage of twenty-five years, Tim and I have both had to adapt to the changes in each other's faith, dreams, opinions, and activities. When you fully commit to a relationship with God, you're making the same kind of commitment. For better or for worse. In sickness and in health. For richer and for poorer. Forevermore. The goal of a loving relationship is to build something strong enough to withstand every one of the as-yet-unknown obstacles.

Easier said than done, right? Even with the best of intentions. Because in your relationship with God—just like in a marriage—you may get bored. That can be enough of an obstacle, but let's face reality here: That's just one of many possible hurdles. You might be angry and resentful. Hurt. You may feel misunderstood or as though you're not being heard. You may get tired of trying. You may think you don't deserve to have what you want.

And at those times, if you want the relationship to get better—and to become stronger—you have to try something new. If you've developed a strong base, it may not be hard to mend the strain on your relationship. It just takes time and some effort. Other times, if you've let it go too long (or faced more than you know how to handle), you'll need to go to great lengths to overcome the troubles that trip you up. In relationships, in life, in prayer.

With that in mind, this week we're going to stretch ourselves. Expand our definition of prayer even further than we already have. Try new things in an attempt to break out of a rut.

You may never have to make a drastic change to breathe new life into your faith, but even if you do, don't be afraid. We've already faced fear. We know God is there and can be trusted. We've sat in silence and colored and written and pondered. This week is about finding new ways to seek God. It's about having some fun in order to build something deeper and stronger.

Communication is always the key to working through issues. And if your prayer life is in need of help, you're in luck— because prayer is, quite simply, communication. If you spend time praying, you will be improving your communication, which in turn improves your relationship. Simply by showing up and putting in time, you're certain to see change. It isn't always easy, but it's always worth it.

 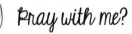

Heavenly Father, I don't want my relationship with You to grow dull. I want to step away from things that are repetitive and stagnant in exchange for a relationship that is fresh and intense and full of life. Fulfilling. Unique. Designed just for me. Something of my very own. But I need Your help. Teach me to turn to You, keeping my mind open to whatever You have for me. Show me ways to work around obstacles—whether severe, like health problems or serious loss, or something as unglamorous as boredom. Keep my faith alive, and give me a new kind of encounter with You—because I'm committed to building a relationship with You that will last. Amen.

REFLECTION QUESTIONS

What changes have you made in your other relationships (with your spouse, children, parents, friends, or coworkers) in order to revive them?

Are you bored with your prayer life? What part(s)?

Have you tried in the past to change it? Were your efforts successful? What happened?

DAY
2

Your Gift to God

*Whatever is good and perfect is a gift coming
down to us from God our Father.*

—JAMES 1:17

God's gifts to us are abundant. He has given us more than we can wrap our minds around. Today, why don't you offer something of yourself back to Him?

DIRECTIONS: Start with a square piece of paper (cut two and a half inches off the end of a piece of letter-sized paper, or use construction paper, gift wrap, or a newspaper). In the center of the page, write something you'd like to offer to God. It can be a heartfelt statement of praise, an acknowledgment of a skill or talent He gave you and an idea about how to use that for Him, or whatever you want. Now google "origami box" for step-by-step instructions—there are plenty of sites to choose from. Then fold your paper into a gift box, following the instructions provided.

As you pray, hold the box in the air and imagine God reaching down to receive it. Keep it beside your bed or on your desk as a reminder to offer yourself and your abilities to Him every day.

EXPLORE | PRAY | WRITE | DRAW

PRAYER PROMPT • • • Pray for someone who
has given you a gift, large or small.

Key Chain Prayers

Never stop praying.
—1 Thessalonians 5:17

"**I** don't have time to pray!" you[1] declare, a teensy bit self-importantly. Until you happen across a quote like this one from Martin Luther, who was asked about his plans for the following day: "Work, work, from early until late. In fact, I have so much to do that I shall spend the first three hours in prayer."

"I don't have three hours," you say, slightly defensively.

But what if you did?

Most of us have more to do than we have time to do it; more events than will fit in the little squares on the calendar. At first glance (or even second and third), we don't have a three-hour block of time available. But who says they have to happen all at once, or even in the same place? Take advantage of those random minutes you spend in the driver's seat—headed to and from the grocery, waiting in line to pick up the kids, driving to meetings and appointments, when you stop and pump gas—by using them for prayer.

As you pass a poster for a lost dog, pray for the family who's missing it. When you see a sign about an upcoming benefit, pray for the needs of the recipient. And as you sit between destinations, waiting for lights to change or your passengers to get into the car, flip through these key chain prayers. Before you know it,

---

[1]By you, I really mean me.

you'll be wishing you had another stop to make so you can have more time to pray.

When you gather all of these stolen moments, you'll be amazed how much you've found.

DIRECTIONS: Cut some index cards or card stock into narrow rectangles the size of a business card or smaller, then use a hole punch to make a hole near one end. Attach them to a binder ring to create a "key chain." You may add them to your actual key chain or make it a separate ring to keep within easy reach. When you hear of prayer needs, add them to the ring, and flip through them in those moments. Use your prayer symbols from page 83 for privacy.

PRAY | WRITE | DRAW | EXPLORE

PRAYER PROMPT • • • Pray for anyone you see driving a black car today.

Set Free

RELATED BIBLE VERSES:
Isaiah 43:1; Psalm 71:23; 1 Timothy 2:5-6

I will shout for joy and sing your praises, for you have ransomed me.
—Psalm 71:23

There have been plenty of TV crime shows and movies about people who have been kidnapped. Inevitably, their loved ones do reckless and frantic things in order to come up with the ransom money. If they can pull together enough cash—or whatever the story line demands—the prisoner will be released. Set free.

Most of us, thank goodness, will never experience this situation firsthand.

And yet, every one of us has a debt we cannot begin to repay. But Someone has already offered to cover everything for us. We don't have to stress about this or feel guilty—just accept it. By His very definition, God is holy and perfect. We are not, which is why Jesus did something that we couldn't do for ourselves. He paid what was necessary to get us back. To set us free.

In theological language, you can say that Jesus ransomed us from sin by dying on the cross on our behalf. In practical terms, that means that we are free. Free from the punishment we deserve. Rescued from captivity. Allowed to stand before God, face-to-face, without fear of judgment. All because of an exchange that Jesus offered to make for us.

DIRECTIONS: Find an old magazine, catalog, or newspaper. (Alternatively, print pages from some colorful magazine websites, or use scrapbooking letters and stickers.) Paste together letters and words to spell out Psalm 71:23 (previous page), and as you create, ask God to let the reality of this kind of love sink deep into your soul.

SAMPLE

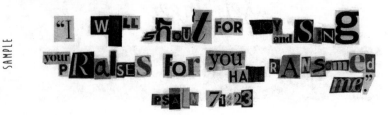

WRITE | DRAW | EXPLORE | PRAY

PRAYER PROMPT ・・・ Thank God for freedom—for our country, for a person who's been incarcerated, for an attorney who defended someone you know, for freedom to worship as we wish, or for someone who sacrificed his or her life in order to preserve our freedom.

Singing His Praises

Sing a new song to the LORD! Let the whole earth sing to the LORD!
—PSALM 96:1

DIRECTIONS: Put together a playlist of songs containing each word from this verse. You can search your own music, look through a streaming service, or browse YouTube or Google. Write your song titles on the lines provided, circling the key words. As you listen to music, open your heart to new revelations and insights about God and faith and prayer. Let this exercise be your song of praise today. Save your playlist and listen to it when you sit down to pray.

SING _____

A _____

NEW _____

SONG _____

TO _____

THE _____

LORD _____

LET _____

THE _____

WHOLE _____

EARTH _____

SING _____

TO _____

THE _____

LORD _____

DRAW | EXPLORE | PRAY | WRITE

PRAYER PROMPT ... Pray for your favorite musician (someone you know or someone famous).

Poetic Praise

Poetry is a language in which man explores his own amazement.
—CHRISTOPHER FRY

$\mathcal{A}$lthough I'm a writer, something inside makes me want to run away, screaming in fear, at the thought of trying to write poetry. I am convinced it's over my head and that I can't properly understand it, which is only true part of the time. I do know, though, that one of the things that makes poetry powerful is its careful choice of words. A good poet will consider rhythm and symbolism and nuance to select the perfect word to convey the depth of his or her meaning. Every word is deliberate. In that sense, writing poetry can be difficult. But it's not impossible.

Haiku is a traditional Japanese form of poetry consisting of three lines. The first contains five syllables, followed by seven, and then five. I remember writing these in elementary school—they're short, and the syllables are measurable, so they aren't as formidable as some other types of poetry. In fact, they seem perfectly approachable—think of them as friendly poems.

I'll go first:

> *I cast my thoughts up*
> *Beg You to catch them, and then—*
> *Confidently wait.*

DIRECTIONS: Now it's your turn. Remember: five, seven, five. Feel free to try several until you feel as though you've captured the essence of your prayer. And then read it aloud to God.

EXPLORE | PRAY | WRITE | DRAW

PRAYER PROMPT • • • Pray for someone with abilities different than yours (a poet, musician, chef, engineer, dancer, filmmaker, surgeon).

DAY
7

(DAY OF REST)

a Blank Canvas

RELATED BIBLE VERSE:
Philippians 4:8

Every day is an opportunity to be creative—the canvas is your mind,
the brushes and colours are your thoughts and feelings, the panorama
is your story, the complete picture is a work of art called 'my life.'
Be careful what you put on the canvas of your mind today—it matters.

—INNERSPACE

*a*ll too easily our thoughts are waylaid. We start to notice the
things that are wrong rather than what is right. We become
critical, jealous, discontent. But there's a simple way to turn your
thoughts upside down—focus on something new. Something
lovely. Something pure.

DIRECTIONS: Fill your mind today with only that which is beautiful.
Uplifting. Enlightening. Holy. If you'd like to draw or paint it, grab a canvas
or draw on the canvas on the next page.

PRAY | WRITE | DRAW | EXPLORE

PRAYER PROMPT••• Pray for someone who creates beautiful things.

How to Pray When Life Is Messy

RELATED BIBLE VERSES:
Hebrews 12:1; Psalm 40

He will take great delight in you,
he will quiet you with his love.
—ZEPHANIAH 3:17

One must learn an inner solitude, wherever one may be.
—MEISTER ECKHART

Today I am not the most shining example of mother-hood. The sun is shining but I am certainly not. I yelled at my fourteen-year-old son at 5:45 a.m. when he didn't want to wake up for morning soccer practice and then cried myself back to sleep. I tried to have a discussion with my twenty-one-year-old about a simple chore I've asked her to do for weeks, with no success, and it ended with both of us shouting and me screaming at her, grabbing my bag, and leaving the house in tears. It sounds stupid. And it is. But that doesn't change the fact that I'm fuming mad and not feeling all that loving or prayerful right now.

This comes amid two months of summer scheduling chaos, a rapidly approaching book deadline, and the highest number of hours I've billed for work in months. My husband is also working really long hours, and I feel like I'm holding down the fort all by myself. It comes in a time of late-paying clients and a stack of unpaid bills on my desk. Of transitioning from having just one child at home to a summer break—meaning my two college-aged girls are back with all their independence and piles of *stuff* in every corner.

My friend Peggy had the misfortune of calling with some good news, and I pulled myself together long enough to rejoice with her before spilling all of today's drama and emotion on her. I said, "I was planning to leave the house to write this afternoon, and now I'm gone, but I'm not in any frame of mind to go *pray* now."

As always, she spoke wisdom and truth to me. "Honey, you're in exactly the frame of mind. Write about prayer right now, and then pray. People don't want to know about prayer when everything is good. They want to know how to deal with it when life is in the crapper."

So here I am.

Let me assure you, I know these are not life-and-death situations. So many of the things we face daily are huge. True loss, severe and unavoidable consequences, serious and real stuff that far surpasses stress- and hormone-induced rage.

It's never just *one* situation that makes it hard to pray, but an accumulation. Emotions and losses. Disappointments and mistakes. Look at any given day, and you'll see this one thing that got on your nerves. Another that distracted you. One that waylaid you. And each of those connects to the thing that happened last time, and the time before that. There will be lots of *next* ones too. It's not realistic to think that we'll ever be without pain or fear or grief or doubt or chaos.

We need God *now*, every single day, each and every moment, not at some unforeseeable point in the future. Not only in the moments of crisis, but in the days in between.

The *only* way to get through anything—to get through *everything*—is to pray.

Fine, but *how?* What practical steps can I take to pray when I'm _____ ? (In pain. Sad. Depressed. When God isn't answering or I'm not inspired. When I'm out of words. When life is hard. You fill in the blank.)

In an ideal world, I would turn to God first. Always.

But I'm more likely to text a friend or buy a new pair of shoes to distract myself. Or run out of the house sobbing after yelling at my kids. I tend to cry first, vent second, and then realize I've done it all backwards and turn to Him feeling ashamed at how messed up I am.

And when I do turn to Him, I can't make my mind stop whirring. I can't stop hearing the chaos and noise of life. I need silence to drown out the noise.

So I sit. I imagine the whirring gears in my mind slowing, then stopping. I focus on stilling my entire body. I close my eyes and begin. "Lord . . ." I take a deep breath, and I feel anxiety fluttering again, so I take another. I don't even try to find words. I soak in the presence of God. Knowing that whatever is ailing me, He can fix. Whatever is lost can be restored. Whatever troubles me can be managed.

I wait for calm to flood my soul. Wait for my sense of equilibrium to be restored.

And it will happen, if I wait. If I still my mind and heart and body and reach out toward God.

I realize that I don't have control—boy, do I *not* have control—over so many situations in my life. But I also remember that I'm not alone. I've fought through some major trials in my faith. I've experienced serious financial hardships, relationship issues, parenting problems, and faced my most hated of earthly diseases, cancer. My dad is in remission, and my mother-in-law is cured—but I lost my father-in-law less than a week ago and lost my mom four years ago. My faith in a good God was buried with her. It took years of baby steps to find my way back—but I did. One step, one deep breath, one quiet moment at a time.

But with each new loss, I fall backwards a bit. I think we all do.

There's some good news, though, for all of us.

Even when *we* are not faithful, God remains faithful.

As long as I turn back, He'll offer me more. He is there when I seek Him again. I have to make that first step—but He never withholds Himself or holds grudges.

I certainly don't mean to oversimplify the process, but the truth is that something supernatural happens when we long for Him. When we pray. When we recognize our own limitations, when we acknowledge the barriers before us. When we ask God to quiet our souls and renew our strength.

Pray with me?

Prince of Peace, I find myself unable to cope with life sometimes. Instead of feeling grateful, I feel bogged down by the responsibilities of all that You've given me. I want to live out Your love, but I find myself consumed with frustration, jealousy, or worry. I want to grow closer to You, but in practice, I'm too tired or bored or busy. Circumstances will rarely be ideal; I know that. But I also know that the only thing that makes life worthwhile is living it with You. Show me how to pray when things aren't perfect. Show me how to put aside all of the weights and sins and emotions that tangle me up. And demonstrate to me, daily, the reality that if I spend time with You, things will be better. I will be better. Amen.

REFLECTION QUESTIONS

What aspects of your life, schedule, or personality make it difficult for you to pray?

How do you quiet your mind when life gets messy?

Have you ever turned away from God? What happened when you came back? How did you feel?

How to Pray When You Want to Go Deeper

My three prayers are variations on Help, Thanks, Wow. That's all I ever need, besides the silence, the pain, and the pause sufficient for me to stop, close my eyes, and turn inward.
—ANNE LAMOTT, *HELP, THANKS, WOW*

*M*any prayers can be simplified into one word or thought. Anne Lamott believes those three words are *help*, *thanks*, and *wow*. One of my most ubiquitous prayers is along those same lines—*please*. Just because the need prompting it can be simplified does not mean the prayer is shallow. Your one word can be your whole prayer—or just the beginning. If you start there and explore, you can add layers and depths of color—like a detailed painting versus a quick, scribbled sketch.

DIRECTIONS: Think of what you need to pray about today, then ask God to help you sum that up in one word. It can be *help*, *thanks*, or *wow*, or one of your own—*healing, hope, support, life, justice, peace, love, comfort.*

Write or doodle your word here: _____

Now we're going to explore—and discover—the power behind that one word.

Look up a definition of your word, and write it here.

_____

What other words come to mind when you think of it?

_____

If your Bible has an index in the back, see if the word is listed there, or search a Bible website for instances of that word. Jot down some of the verses that relate to it. Look them up and read any accompanying notes. Mark any that seem to apply to your situation.

Now, using one of those verses, pray. Remind God of the time in the Bible when He said this, or when Jesus did that, or when someone else drew near to Him. Ask Him to do the same for you. As you color in the words below, consider each one prayerfully.

WRITE | DRAW | EXPLORE | PRAY

PRAYER PROMPT • • • Pray for the first person who comes to mind when you hear each word: kindness, generosity, encouragement, determination, hope.

How to Pray When the World Overwhelms You

RELATED BIBLE VERSES:
Romans 8:37; John 16:33

I have told you all this so that you may have peace in
me. Here on earth you will have many trials and sorrows.
But take heart, because I have overcome the world.

—JOHN 16:33

Call me an ostrich, if you will, because I spend more time with my head buried in the sand than above it. When I read or watch the news, my soul withers. My heart hurts, and sorrow overwhelms me. Not all news is bad, of course, but that seems to be what is always emphasized. I need to remember—and maybe you do too—that although we will face all kinds of horrific things, devastation does not get the final word. God does. He triumphs in the end, and we have to hold on to that truth, whatever horrors or evils we witness.

DIRECTIONS: Pick up a newspaper and a magic marker. As you skim the stories, let yourself feel anger or grief, sadness or righteous indignation. But don't let yourself get bogged down by despair, because God is bigger than every single one of these stories. Take your marker and pen your prayer right over the stories. *Heal her. Bring hope. Shine Your light. Help me not to despair. Reveal Yourself. Restore. Renew. Fix it, Lord. Show mercy. Bring justice. Redeem lost time. Thank You.*

DRAW | EXPLORE | PRAY | WRITE

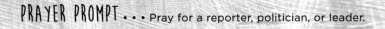

PRAYER PROMPT · · · Pray for a reporter, politician, or leader.

How to Pray When You Can't Keep It All Straight

O Sovereign LORD! You made the heavens and earth by your
strong hand and powerful arm. Nothing is too hard for you!
—JEREMIAH 32:17

Prayer would be easy if we just had one problem on our
minds . . . one health issue, one relationship in jeopardy, one child
worrying us, one critical deadline. But the reality is, our lives are
full. They overflow with blessings but they're also jam-packed
with concerns. Eyes that can't unsee things. Minds that can't
forget. Finances that won't stretch far enough. Faith that feels
insufficient.

We're going to take your long list of people and situations that
need God and weave together these stresses, and then we're going
to pull out one at a time and hand each to God. It's not too
much for Him. *He* doesn't need them to be broken apart. We do.

DIRECTIONS: Fold a sheet of colored paper in half. Cut slits in the fold,
about an inch apart, stopping about an inch from the edge of the paper.
Unfold the paper. Now cut some 1-1/2 inch strips of a different colored

paper the same width. Weave the loose strips through the first sheet, going over and under. For the next row, start under and then go over.

Think of all the needs you have—people you love who are struggling, relationships, financial situations, work problems, acquaintances who are ill, friends who are grieving. Write them on the exposed parts of the colored strips of paper. I like to group similar needs on the same strips (prayers for my children, health-related prayers, etc.).

Now carefully slide out one strip at a time, saying a brief prayer over each concern. When you're finished, slide the strip back into place—with the writing facing down. When we hand our worries over to God, it clears our minds and allows us to face each situation one at a time. The need hasn't evaporated, but you've placed it in the hands of God. And there's no better place for it to be.

EXPLORE | PRAY | WRITE | DRAW

PRAYER PROMPT • • • Pray for someone who
has more going on than you do.

How to Pray When Your Need Seems Impossible

RELATED BIBLE VERSES:
Matthew 19:26; Luke 1:37;
Matthew 17:20; Jeremiah 32:27

"There's no use trying," [Alice] said.
"One can't believe impossible things."
"I daresay you haven't had much practice," said the Queen. "When I
was your age, I always did it for half an hour a day. Why, sometimes
I've believed as many as six impossible things before breakfast."
—LEWIS CARROLL, *ALICE'S ADVENTURES IN WONDERLAND*

I don't know about you, but I find myself treating God as though I can decide on His behalf what He will or won't do, which things are reasonable requests and which are asking too much.

It's funny, really, when you think about it. When did I decide I know more than God? What makes me think I have that kind of power over what He does?

God is not limited—by anything, any time or power or ability. He can do all things. It doesn't mean that He *will*. Just that He is able. We cannot constrain or restrict Him.

Impossible is a word *we* use, not one He uses.

Think about that one prayer request that feels impossible to you—it may be overwhelming, scary, or something you want God to do but don't think He will.

DIRECTIONS: What is your impossible-seeming prayer? Write it here.

Remind God of the reasons you know He is able—based on what you have personally experienced, what you have seen Him do for others, or what you know about God and His nature. Write those reasons here.

Look over your reminders about God's ability to answer your prayer. Now revise your impossible prayer here, praying and believing that it is entirely possible for God to do what you need.

PRAY | WRITE | DRAW | EXPLORE

PRAYER PROMPT • • • Pray for someone who's already
received an incredible or unbelievable answer to prayer
(even if you don't know him or her personally).

How to Pray When You Need a Fresh Point of View

What we do see depends mainly on what we look for. . . .
In the same field the farmer will notice the crop, the geologists
the fossils, botanists the flowers, artists the colouring, sportmen
the cover for the game. Though we may all look at the same
things, it does not all follow that we should see them.
—JOHN LUBBOCK,
THE BEAUTIES OF NATURE AND THE WONDERS OF THE WORLD WE LIVE IN

When I travel, I always pack a camera. On some trips, I've taken more than a thousand photos. (The advent of digital photography has saved me a fortune in film developing costs.) With all that time behind the lens, you'd think it would significantly slow me down. But the delays are slight.

As I walk along, my eye is constantly evaluating the scene before me, like a moving viewfinder. I watch for the way the buildings and coastlines and hills and shadows align with one another. Since I'm always on the lookout, I can gauge quickly at which point to take the photo. Sometimes I have to step back to an earlier spot, but I've gotten pretty good at predicting at which angles the scene will look best.

If you stand in a different spot than I do, we will see different things.

In life, even if we stand in exactly the same spot, our experiences, backgrounds, and personalities will cause us to see the same situation in a different way. It's why Steve Jobs envisioned sleek, simple designs while others didn't. It's why a Picasso painting looks very different from a Rembrandt. In prayer, it can be helpful to try to look at your need from someone else's point of view. It may help you notice an answer you'd missed or see a possibility you hadn't recognized.

DIRECTIONS: Fill in the chart on the next page, beginning with your need at the top. On the left side, add the names of a variety of people, and then in the space to the right, jot down how each of them might see your situation. When you're done, close your eyes and pray . . . as yourself . . . now that you've looked at it in new ways.

YOUR SITUATION OR NEED

PEOPLE, REAL OR FICTIONAL, FRIENDS OR STRANGERS. *{Examples: Mother Teresa, the president of the United States, a local politician, Jane Austen, a football coach, a grandmother, a preschooler, your best friend.}*	**HOW MIGHT EACH PERSON LOOK AT YOUR SITUATION?**

WRITE | DRAW | EXPLORE | PRAY

PRAYER PROMPT ... Pray for someone who holds a different opinion than you do (in politics, religion, morality, or leadership).

(DAY OF REST)

How to Pray When You're Tired

Be still, and know that I am God!
—PSALM 46:10

Distraught, I stood in the receiving line following my mom's memorial service. She died after fighting small-cell lung cancer for three years, and I suppose it goes without saying that knowing it was coming didn't make it any easier. I'd lost my mom, and I didn't think anything would ever be right again. Even through my fog of grief, though, one moment stands out in its beauty. Gary Mosbaugh, a former (and favorite) teacher who had worked with Mom, stood before me. He looked me in the eyes and gave me a long hug. He pulled back, not saying a word, and looked at me again before moving on. It was one of the most meaningful, pure, and quiet conversations I've ever had.

DIRECTIONS: Psalm 46:10 says to be still. So today, let this awareness fill the air around you. Close your eyes and simply breathe Him in. He's right there. Right now. The NASB translates "Be still" as "Cease striving." In other words, stop working. You don't have to earn His love. You can't. You already have it. Simply rest in the knowledge that He is God, and let yourself feel whatever that makes you feel. It may be the most beautiful conversation you've ever had with Him. Then color the following page in your favorite hues.

DRAW | EXPLORE | PRAY | WRITE

Designed to Live in Full Color

RELATED BIBLE VERSES:
Exodus 24:16; Exodus 34:29; Matthew 5:16; John 1:5

The Lord—who is the Spirit—makes us more and more like him as we are changed into his glorious image.
—2 CORINTHIANS 3:18

Winter in Indiana isn't always beautiful. When the snow drifts just right, and the winter sunlight glints off the snow-covered branches, and when you take time to notice that the shadows from the corn stubble left in the field are a lovely bluish-purple, then yes, it can be called pretty. As long as you're able to stay warm. But much of the time, our winter landscape consists of drab browns— grass and weeds and plants that are dead and dry and crumbly, washed-out gray skies, and the stark skeletal tree branches, bare of leaves, silhouetted against the sky.

One morning as I drove to meet a friend for lunch, the scenery took my breath away.

A dense white fog had settled onto the ground in the night, and though it had cleared in most areas, it left behind a beautiful frost. Everything was covered. The crystals outlined each blade of grass, the fence posts and wires, the individual pine needles, the bushes and the plants and every single delicate branch of the trees. It was breathtaking. Suddenly, the blah landscape was transformed into a thing of remarkable beauty. All around me was a shade of white, with the lightest, purest white coming from the sun, trying to burn through the fog. Bluish-whites and grayish-whites and dull whites and sparkly whites; it was like looking at a magical, make-believe world.

It was the same view that had been there the night before, the same as it had been all winter—except for one thing. The frost. That one little touch—that specific combination of temperatures and humidity and cloud cover and air pressure—made all the difference in the world. Suddenly, I was able to see everything in a new way. In a way that highlighted its intricate design.

The frost itself was virtually without color. Clear, or in some places, white. It wasn't the color of the frost that made it beautiful—it was the light.

The Bible equates God to light. *The light shines in the darkness. Let there be light. Jesus is the light of man.*

Without light, we cannot see beauty—really, we cannot see at all. When light isn't present, we cannot distinguish color; it has no impact in the dark. Jesus came to bring us out of darkness and into the light. The seven colors on the visible light spectrum (often referred to as Roy G. Biv—red, orange, yellow, green, blue, indigo, and violet) are, in reality, reflected rays of light. The objects don't contain the colors; what we see is the light that is not absorbed.

As God draws us into the light of His love, all those things we'd rather keep hidden become known. That means they also lose their power—no more secrets, no more unknown. God's light is truth. We don't have to be held back by what is in our past. In the book of Isaiah, we're told, "Forget the former things; do not dwell on the past" (Isaiah 43:18, NIV).

We're all products of our environment, if we let ourselves be. When Moses went up on the mountain to receive the Commandments, the glory of God settled there in the form of a cloud. When Moses came down the mountain, he wasn't the same because the Spirit of God changed him. How quickly we all pick up the prevailing mood or spirit—when good things happen, our outlook is positive and hopeful; when we're confronted with trouble or anger or hatred, we respond in kind. In other words, we are changed, just as the landscape was—but are we changed in a good way?

If we immerse ourselves in the glory of God, if we let Him saturate our days, our minds, and our spirits, then His beauty will cling to us. His magnificence will outline our very beings, and we'll walk around transformed. People will see our individual attributes and formerly hidden beauty. But if we don't surround ourselves with His presence, if we don't allow His grace and mercy and love to permeate us, nothing will change. We'll still remain drab, dull, and (frankly) not all that interesting.

Just as frost can transform a landscape, colors can transform your prayer life. This week, we're going to discover the inherent properties within some individual colors. Not to sound overly dramatic, but while we're on the subject, can I confess something to you? I think God created color just for me. Because I can't imagine anyone loving it more. I love to cover my walls with the perfect shades and simply sit—wrapped in it, surrounded by color. It soothes me, inspires me, energizes me. It illuminates the deepest part of me and wakes up something inside.

Perhaps it's because it comes from our abundant, colorful God, and He designed us in His image.

As we learn about different colors, we're going to pray for God to unlock those attributes within us. Pay attention to the color that seems to match your natural personality most closely, and notice colors that represent traits you don't have or struggle with. Watch for strokes of these colors to manifest in your life, and see what you can learn through them.

Before long, you'll notice nuances you've never seen before. Vibrancy you only imagined. God's colorful presence pervading every hour, every moment. Because He didn't design us for a drab, monotonous life. He created us to live life in full color.

Pray with me?

Without You, life is dull and boring, filled with dark shadows and monotony. But with You, Lord, life is vibrant and radiant. Wash over me, transforming me into the work of art You designed me to be. Like Moses, I want to be changed by my experience with You. My life is Your canvas, God. Help me reflect all the colors of Your love, all the magnificence of Your light. And help me to watch for Your colorful beauty in every moment of my day. Amen.

REFLECTION QUESTIONS

Without looking ahead at the characteristics associated with each color, answer the following: What is your favorite color? Why?

Which color least appeals to you? Why?

Describe the most beautiful, colorful aspect of nature that you've seen (in photos or real life).

Now think about what that teaches you about God, who wasn't content to create this world in just black and white.

DAY 2

Passionate Red

RELATED BIBLE VERSES:
Psalm 73:25-26; 1 John 4:7-8

You must love the LORD your God with all your heart,
all your soul, all your mind, and all your strength.
—MARK 12:30

RED: Passion. Heat. Fire. Energy. Signifying emotional intensity, red increases respiration rate and raises blood pressure. It's aggressive and energetic. Extreme. Bold and vivid and sure.

Loving God, we're starting this colorful prayer journey with red. Renew my passion. Let me long for You as desperately as You desire. Pursue me as I pour my energies into finding more of You—learning about You, drawing close to You, feeling the heat of Your embrace, the intensity of Your love. It's fitting that red is the color of blood and of love, because both, together, represent the reality of the sacrifice You made for me— without my asking or even knowing I needed it. You are passionate and expansive in the ways You love me. Help me to see, to understand (even just a little bit) the all-consuming and never-ending love You have for me—for each and every one of us. And give us the courage to welcome it, accept it, and embrace it. In all its vibrancy, all its passion. Amen.

DIRECTIONS: Quick! Write a love letter to God in the heart frame. Don't stop to think about it. Just pour out whatever is in your heart. Pull from the deepest depths of your emotions. Grab a red pen or marker and get started! Write urgently and passionately and quickly. Go!

EXPLORE | PRAY | WRITE | DRAW

PRAYER PROMPT • • • Pray for someone who faces emergencies regularly (firefighter, police officer, nurse, EMT).

Yellow's Joyful Energy

RELATED BIBLE VERSES:
John 8:12; Philippians 4:4; John 15:11

*The LORD God is our sun and our shield. He gives us grace and glory.
The LORD will withhold no good thing from those who do what is right.
O LORD of Heaven's Armies, what joy for those who trust in you.*
—PSALM 84:11-12

*Y*ELLOW: Sunshine and joy, happiness and energy, warmth
and cheerfulness. A spontaneous color, yellow is lighthearted,
fun, and optimistic. Because it's so bright, it commands notice.
Associated with intellect and wisdom.

*Lord, You are the light of the world. So many people think that serving
You is dull and dreary, rigid and limiting. But I've learned that listening to You and looking for You brings joy, a deep and abiding energy. It's
fun to serve You. Spontaneous. Full of surprises and never fading. Like
the flowers that instinctively turn their faces toward the sun, let me turn
my face toward Your light. Let me open my heart to You. Light up my
days. Illuminate the lives of all those around me. And flood our souls
with the warmth of Your love. Amen.*

DIRECTIONS: Joy seems to radiate outward, just as the sun's light reaches far and wide to illuminate everything around it. Today, let gratitude prevail, and write on the spiral the things in your life that bring you joy.

PRAY | WRITE | DRAW | EXPLORE

PRAYER PROMPT • • • Say a silent prayer for everyone you see who is smiling today.

DAY
4

Blue—Safe and Secure

RELATED BIBLE VERSES:
1 John 4:18; Joshua 1:9; Proverbs 18:10; Isaiah 26:3

What if the very constraints on your life, which defeat and frustrate you, which you try to rebel against to no avail, have been placed on your life because they are good? What if the constraints on your life were there to actually make your life beautiful? What if you learned that even the mistakes that have marked your life can be redeemed? What if you learned, rather than to be defeated by the lines that have been marked on your life, to color inside the lines? . . . God tells us to color inside the lines; that our lives will be better if we stay inside the lines He has drawn.
—MATT APPLING, *LIFE AFTER ART*

BLUE: Solid and stable, the color of trust and loyalty. It slows our metabolisms and brings a feeling of calm, serenity, tranquility, and peace. From a spiritual perspective, blue is the color of heaven and authority. Blue reminds us that God has freed us from the hundreds of requirements in the law of the Old Testament and simplified it for us by condensing it to these: Love the Lord with all your heart, and love your neighbor as yourself. While you're at it, maybe you can also color inside the lines.

God of Peace, like the depths of the ocean and the enormity of the sky, Your presence surrounds me without end. I spend most of my days running from one thing to the next, juggling activities and commitments and other people's needs. Left to my own devices, I go through my days feeling frantic, frazzled—You designed me to live in peace, and instead I'm filling my days with busyness. But when I slow my breathing, when I calm my mind, I find that You are right there. In that place, that serene place, I discover peace. I find You. Power and authority. The deepest of loves, the purest of hopes, the epitome of balance. Today, let me feel Your presence washing over me in long, slow waves—drowning out uncertainty, washing away worries, flooding me with peace. Amen.

DIRECTIONS: As you color this abstract image in shades of blue, reflect on the peace that comes from following God and respecting His boundaries.

WRITE | DRAW | EXPLORE | PRAY

PRAYER PROMPT • • • Pray for anyone who works with color—a hairstylist, baker, art teacher, fashion retailer, house painter, or home decorator.

DAY
5

Green Pastures

RELATED BIBLE VERSES:
Matthew 9:36; Psalm 51:10;
Isaiah 40:31; Psalm 96:11-12

*Y*ou're probably familiar with the Twenty-third Psalm, but reading it in a different Bible translation may shine a light on it that you hadn't noticed before.

> The Eternal is my shepherd, He cares for me always.
> He provides me rest in rich, green fields
>   beside streams of refreshing water.
> He soothes my fears;
> He makes me whole again,
>   steering me off worn, hard paths
>   to roads where truth and righteousness echo His name.
> PSALM 23:1–3, THE VOICE

GREEN: The color of nature and nurturing, symbolizing life, growth, freshness, and fertility. It's no coincidence that people head outside to refresh themselves. Green is quieting and renewing, connoting safety, stability, and endurance. It can also represent newness or inexperience.

Lord, You are my shepherd. You are the safe haven in which I can find renewal. While I reside there, in the lush grove of Your unconditional love, help me to rest. To rest in the newness of life that You bring, the renewal of my soul. In this peaceful place with You, let me know that I am safe. You are a peaceful sanctuary, the peaceful sanctuary, bringing experience to counter my inexperience. New growth to replace the old. Life to restore what is dead or broken inside. Today, Lord, help me to rest in this fertile place, this place where anything is possible and life is abundant and rich. Amen.

DIRECTIONS: Select two or three familiar Bible verses, and look them up in at least three different translations. Write them in the spaces provided on these pages. Be open to seeing something new, to breathing new life into verses you may know by heart. Look at them all together to get a fuller understanding of their meaning.

DRAW | EXPLORE | PRAY | WRITE

PRAYER PROMPT ••• Pray for someone who has been made to lie down and rest (a pregnant woman on bed rest, someone with a sports injury, a grouchy toddler).

Dreaming in Purple

RELATED BIBLE VERSES:
Acts 2:17; Ephesians 3:20; Romans 12:6

PURPLE: With the energy of red and the integrity of blue, purple (also called violet) represents imagination and dreams, a link between the physical and spiritual. Ambitious and self-assured, violet shows creativity and imagination, inspiration and originality, and traditionally has been used to depict royalty.

Ruler of All, Your originality and creativity are unending. You've given me the ability to dream big and without limits. But no dream I have will ever fulfill me if You're not the One inspiring it, the driving force and the creative energy behind it. Help me to see that You really are in all things. Just as purple is the combination of these two colors, You are both the passion and love of red and the stability and strength of blue. You provide imagination and desire. Help me dream, Lord, with the magnitude and vision befitting of a child of the King of kings. Let Your dreams for me become my own. And provide all that I need to make them come true. Amen.

DIRECTIONS: What are your dreams? What do you want to accomplish? Draw, write, sketch, plan, or diagram some of your thoughts. Use additional pages if you wish—don't be afraid to dream big!

DEAR LORD,

THESE ARE MY DREAMS.

HELP ME TO . . .

EXPLORE | PRAY | WRITE | DRAW

PRAYER PROMPT . . . Pray for someone who has appeared in your dreams.

DAY
7

(DAY OF REST)

Color Wheel of Prayer

RELATED BIBLE VERSES:
Matthew 6:33; Philippians 4:19; Colossians 1:15-17

I came that they may have life and have it abundantly.
—JOHN 10:10, ESV

Imagine how boring it would be if we only had one crayon to color with. Fortunately for us, Jesus came so that we could have abundant life—everything we need, all found within Him. He brings fullness of color, newness of life, passion, and energy to our days.

DIRECTIONS: Fill in the sections of the color wheel with the right colors. Then walk through the steps of the prayer wheel, dwelling on putting each color's meaning to use as you approach God. When you reach the last color, purple, ask God for your heart's desire.

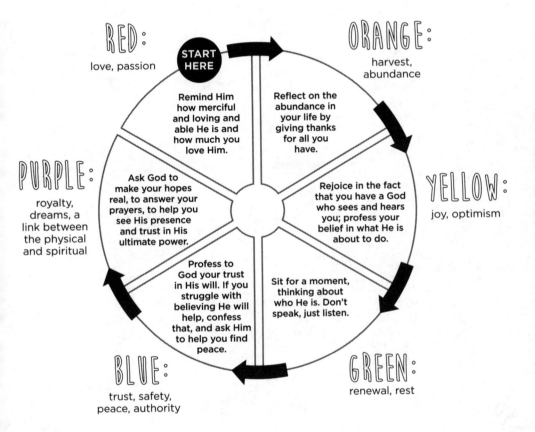

RED:
love, passion

ORANGE:
harvest, abundance

YELLOW:
joy, optimism

GREEN:
renewal, rest

BLUE:
trust, safety, peace, authority

PURPLE:
royalty, dreams, a link between the physical and spiritual

START HERE

Remind Him how merciful and loving and able He is and how much you love Him.

Reflect on the abundance in your life by giving thanks for all you have.

Rejoice in the fact that you have a God who sees and hears you; profess your belief in what He is about to do.

Sit for a moment, thinking about who He is. Don't speak, just listen.

Profess to God your trust in His will. If you struggle with believing He will help, confess that, and ask Him to help you find peace.

Ask God to make your hopes real, to answer your prayers, to help you see His presence and trust in His ultimate power.

PRAY | WRITE | DRAW | EXPLORE

PRAYER PROMPT ••• Pray for someone to achieve their dreams
(an entrepreneur, a child, a college student, a performer).

A BEAUTIFUL BEGINNING

RELATED BIBLE VERSES:
Romans 12:2; Ephesians 4:22-24;
1 Thessalonians 5:23

*Keep putting into practice all you learned and received
from me—everything you heard from me and saw me
doing. Then the God of peace will be with you.*
—PHILIPPIANS 4:9

You may have reached the end of this book, but you're
not finished yet.

The Bible tells us to "Come boldly to the throne of
our gracious God. There we will receive his mercy, and
we will find grace to help us when we need it most"
(Hebrews 4:16). A friend commented to me, "Sometimes,
I think we *need* to come boldly so we can get through all
the obstacles in the way."

It's worth the effort. Because whether we think we
want to change or not, and even if it doesn't change the
outcome, prayer *will* change us.

God promises, as part of the transforming work (or
growth in grace, or spiritual growth) He undertakes when
we follow Him, that we will be set apart and made holy.
And that He won't let go of us until He is done. (Which
is never.) There's always more we can do—and, thank
goodness, there's no end to what He *will* do. If we follow

Jesus, then let's imitate Him. Watch. Observe. Follow. Listen. Go straight to the Source.

And the way we do that? Through prayer.

Hopefully now you know in your head—but, more important, you know deep in your heart—that prayer changes things. By now, you have constructed a broader definition of prayer. A wider understanding. An awareness that there are countless ways to talk to God. And even though there are unlimited ways of putting prayer into practice, in its simplest form, prayer is simply communicating with God. When life is calm or when you are desperate. In the quiet or surrounded by noise. All by yourself or in the midst of a crowd.

Whatever you need, wherever you are, God is able to provide. He has the answer ready before you know there is a problem.

Just remember to keep looking, to keep believing that the answer will come. And be willing to accept it when it does.

When my friend Suzanne adopted a little girl from China, she was taught that a child's ability to attach to her new parents would depend on whether she had attached to her caregivers, and if she had, she would be upset when she was removed from them. Back at the hotel, all of the other parents' babies were grieving, but Suzanne's daughter, Kristen, was not. She seemed perfectly happy. But after what Suzanne had learned about bonding with her new baby, she was concerned. She wrote to her friend Jill, "I'm worried because she doesn't seem to be grieving. I'm afraid she's not going to be able to attach to us."

Jill replied, "Suzanne, what have you asked of every single person who wanted to pray for you? For the last six months everyone has been praying for God to prepare Kristen's heart to be open to you. Stop looking for something to be wrong. God answered your prayers!"

He did. Kristen is now a well-adjusted ten-year-old who loves her family and friends. But Suzanne almost missed seeing God's hand in that moment because she didn't expect God to give her what she asked for so quickly. It's true that God's answers may not always look the way we expect them to look. Okay, let's face it, they may rarely look that way. But that makes our answered prayers no less real. No less right.

God always responds. He always hears. He always leans toward us, hands extended. Because everything He has for us is wrapped up in our relationships with Him. We can only find it all by turning toward Him. In fact, the only thing He wants more than that is for us to not just turn and not just walk, but to *run*. To never, ever be satisfied and continue to move always closer.

So don't stop here. Keep moving toward our welcoming, generous God. The One who soothes our fears, loves us as our Father, reveals connections and forms relationships, teaches us to love others, knows us personally and specifically, revives our passion, redeems our time, overcomes all of the obstacles we pile up on our way to meet Him, and colors our worlds. He transforms us, changes our perceptions, and offers His complete love to us without condition.

Run, my friend, run. And don't hesitate—because I'm right behind you. God is standing there, expectant, arms open wide. What are we waiting for?

REFLECTION QUESTIONS

Look back at page 4 and read what you wrote at the start of this journey about prayer. Think about what you hoped to discover and what you actually found or experienced, and then answer these questions. Take your time.

In what ways, if any, are you disappointed (in yourself, in prayer, in this book, in God)?

What did you learn (about yourself, about prayer, about God)?

What practices are you going to incorporate from this point forward?

STARTING A RELATIONSHIP WITH GOD

RELATED BIBLE VERSES:
Romans 3:23; John 10:17-18;
Romans 1:4; Romans 8:11

If you openly declare that Jesus is Lord and believe in your heart that God raised him from the dead, you will be saved. For it is by believing in your heart that you are made right with God, and it is by openly declaring your faith that you are saved.
—ROMANS 10:9-10

There are no hoops to jump through and no ten-step checklist I can offer. The whole point of Jesus coming to earth was to show us that salvation is in His hands, not ours. When He died on the cross, He paid for every bit of sin, every temptation we gave into, everything we could ever do wrong. All of it, for all of time, for each and every one of us. It's hard to get your head around that, isn't it? For some of us, it's a hard thing to accept—we didn't ask Him to do that, and it seems extreme. But the truth is, no matter how good we try to be, we are not perfect. And all the ways we fall short of that mark? That's what sin is, and sin puts a wedge between us and God. Because God is holy, and sin (of any kind) is an affront to His perfection. So Jesus willingly—out of His unfathomable love for us—sacrificed Himself to remove any obstacle. No other payment needed. Access granted. There is nothing we can do to earn this gift; all we can do is accept it.

Three days after Jesus died on the cross, He rose again—showing us that death has no power over Him. He continues to live, and He offers that same life to us. The cross wasn't the end, but the beginning. His resurrection is the supreme miracle of Christianity. I know that. But here's how it feels to me: The miracle is that we now have access to Him. All we have to do to have a relationship with God is to ask Him. And He will never say "no," or "not now," or "maybe if you clean up your act." I picture Him leaning forward, in anticipation, tears of joy in His eyes. "Come to Me, My child. I love you."

If you've never invited God into your life, tell Him you want to know Him. You don't have to follow a specific formula. Just use your own words, and let them come from your heart. If you aren't sure what to say but want to take this step, you can pray like this:

My Prayer

Dear Lord, I admit that I am a sinner, and I believe You died on the cross to save me and then rose again to live forevermore. You did something for me that I cannot do for myself, and it's all because of how much You love me. I ask You to forgive me for all I've done wrong, and I accept Your gift of salvation. Come into my life. There's so much I don't know—but I am ready to trust You. Most of all, thank You for loving me. Thank You for wanting me. Thank You for all that You have done for me. In the holy name of Jesus, I pray. Amen.

ONGOING PRAYERS

When my friend Sherry was in a challenging phase of life, facing serious health problems, not to mention big financial concerns and relationship issues, she and her son, Nick, kept a prayer journal. Every day they wrote down a need they had, large or small. From time to time, they reviewed the list and used a yellow highlighter to mark the prayers that had been answered. Later, Sherry joined my prayer group, and we adopted this practice. When we saw God answer prayers, we exclaimed, "I got a yellow!"

Use these pages for your list of prayers, and get your marker ready. Come back here every week or so to pray through the list. If you don't like the color yellow, pick something you do like—because you're going to be seeing a lot of it!

NOTES

Page 2   *God's mercies are renewed daily.* "Great is his faithfulness; his mercies begin afresh each morning." Lamentations 3:23

Page 9   *He already knows the desires of your heart.* "Your Father knows exactly what you need even before you ask him!" Matthew 6:8.

Page 69   *Whatever you do selflessly for others you do for God.* "And the King will say, 'I tell you the truth, when you did it to one of the least of these my brothers and sisters, you were doing it to me!'" Matthew 25:40

Page 73   *But Jesus tells us to pray about everything, and to pray for one another.* "Therefore, confess your sins to one another and pray for one another, that you may be healed. The prayer of a righteous person has great power as it is working." James 5:16, ESV

Page 142   *Even when we are not faithful, God remains faithful.* "If we are unfaithful, he remains faithful, for he cannot deny who he is." 2 Timothy 2:13

Page 144   *Anne Lamott believes those three words are* help, thanks, *and* wow. See Anne Lamott, *Help, Thanks, Wow: The Three Essential Prayers* (New York: Riverhead Books, 2012).

Page 166   *The Bible equates God to light. The light shines in the darkness. Let there be light. Jesus is the light of man.* See John 8:12; John 1:5; Genesis 1:3; and John 1:4.

ACKNOWLEDGMENTS

When I started writing, I thought the writing itself was the gift. Exploring, discovering, becoming. But now I see that writing simply opens the door—what comes after that is the gift. The most valuable and unexpected gift of this writing life is the friendships it has allowed me to develop.

Marcia Kendall, you are one of the loveliest of those friends. Your interest in all things writing, your deep passion for all things faith, and your generous, sparkly, intelligent, and thoughtful spirit make you one of my most treasured friends. I'm so grateful for the way writing deepened our friendship in such a beautiful way.

Nathan and Peg Miller, you inspire me. Always. You continue to model a life of grace and always welcome me with such delight. I love you both.

Joe Roper, Sarah Schmitt, Terri DeVries, Irene Fridsma, Kelsey Timmerman, Jama Kehoe Bigger—the night of my book release party for *Praying Upside Down*, I knew something was missing, but couldn't put my finger on what it was. And then you all walked in and I had exactly what I needed. As wordy as I can be at times, there just aren't enough words to express how grateful I am for your support, inspiration, and steady belief in me. I am better because of my friendship with you.

Tyndale House and The BELONG Tour, I sometimes wonder if I'm dreaming because working with you seems too good to be true. But that's just it—you are good and true, and you let me fully embrace my creative quirks when I work with you. Each individual member of the team brings great value to the process, but I want to especially thank Bonne Steffen. You get me and you make my words shine. I'll never again write "OK" without thinking of you. Blythe Daniel, you epito-mize everything I hoped an agent would be. I'm fortunate to have you believing in me.

Kerry and Doug Dunham, our evenings spent together keep me grounded. (Not that *you* would ever believe I am grounded, but I can't imagine what a mess I'd be without you.)

Rob O'Dell, when God chose you to be my father, it was one of the best gifts I've ever been given. Thank you for being you. And Rita Jerger, thank you for the way you love my dad and our family.

Kris Williams, Wendy Muse, Lynn Schriner, LeeAnne Lehr and Colleese—your texts and e-mails, words and prayers are always just what I need at exactly the right time. God has used you to let me know He is still in this, and I'm thankful.

Suzanne Thompson, Kathryn Schueren, and Julie Baird—I love our Wednesday mornings and our God-centered friendship. And I love that my pleas for prayer are met earnestly and immediately with every text I send you.

Richard Merriman (the first person I described this book to, long before I knew I even got to write it), Lisa Wheeler, Sherry Boyle, Sharon Rapoport, Tami Sells, Michelle Moore, Goyita Young, Vickie Bollman, Robert and Andrea Miller—I love you all. You've inspired me in countless ways, and you make my life richer.

Katie, Anna, and Bobby, sometimes I think I'm a terrible mom—I'm busy, distracted, and not always fun to be around. And then I look at you and I see vivacious, interesting, talented people beginning to find their own ways in this world, and I think maybe I haven't done too badly. Tim, I don't know what I did to earn your unwavering devotion, but I'd be lost without you believing in me. I love you.

And You, Lord. You knew my desires long before I did, and You have clearly walked beside me, holding me up when I am weak, sending friends when I feel lost, and giving me insights when I turn to You. I couldn't do this without You, and to be honest, I wouldn't want to. Whether or not I ever publish another word, thank You for letting me connect with You through my writing. You are my light and my source and my hope. I could want nothing more.

ABOUT THE AUTHOR

Kelly O'Dell Stanley is a graphic designer who writes. Or maybe a writer who also designs. Either way, when she found the place where writing and design intersected, she discovered that was exactly where she wanted to be. The author of *Praying Upside Down* and *Designed to Pray*, Kelly loves to explore prayer and faith in creative ways because she knows that God is the Ultimate Creator. And when she puts her creativity into action, she always discovers more of Him.

Twenty-some years ago, Kelly took a leap of faith and began her own business, doing advertising and marketing for clients across the US. Her work has been included in design anthologies and *PRINT Magazine*'s Design Annual, and she's received awards from the NAHB, Public Relations Society of America, the Webby Competition, and Art Directors Club of Indiana.

Kelly's writing awards include first place in Inspirational Writing in the 2013 *Writer's Digest* competition. She is a regular monthly contributor to Internet Café Devotions and has written for (in)courage, *Today's Christian Woman*, *Today's Christian Living*, *Tiferet Journal*, *Sasee Magazine*, and numerous blogs.

She's a redhead who does a pretty good job of controlling her temper, a strong believer in doing everything to excess, and a professional wrestler of doubt and faith. (Faith always wins, but some days the competition is fierce.) She's been married to Tim for a quarter of a century, which officially makes him a saint. And she loves her three quirky grown-or-nearly-grown kids, Katie, Anna, and Bobby. Even if they do call her all the time. (Or maybe especially because they call her all the time.)

Kelly lives in Crawfordsville, Indiana. You may connect with her on her blog, www.kellyostanley.com, on Facebook (Kelly O'Dell Stanley, Author), or on Twitter (@kellyostanley).

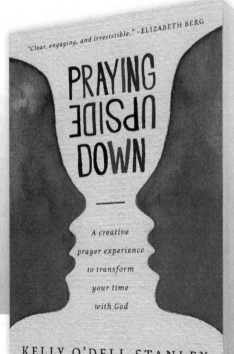

YOU'RE INVITED

To be part of a community of real women who share their struggles and heartaches, hopes and dreams . . . a place where you can settle in and be accepted, just as you are. Join in through the resources below and at BELONGtour.com.

You Belong

An inspiring collection of reflections from a wide variety of women. Stories of identity, purpose, relationships, and living out your faith offer plenty of "me, too" moments. You'll laugh, wipe away an occasional tear, and gain fresh perspective.

Belonging Journal

A space to capture your thoughts, prayers, and dreams. Encouraging verses and insightful quotes from a wide-ranging group of women are sprinkled across lined pages, designed to motivate and inspire you to pour out your heart . . . and explore what it means to belong.

Made to Belong

Go on a six-week journey to discover and pursue your unique calling. In this study of Habakkuk, you'll dig deep, try new things, and step out of your comfort zones as you step into an exciting and fulfilling future.

Designed to Pray

This eight-week adventure is filled with activities—everything from coloring pages to writing prompts to doodling. Here you'll find space to let go of your fears and expectations and discover what it means to engage with the One who loves you.

The BELONG Tour is an experience that challenges women to pursue their best life. It's a call for women of all walks of life and faith to connect more deeply. Get acquainted and find information on events and opportunities to be part of the BELONG community at BELONGtour.com.

CP1102

This is BIG.

Bigger than any one of us. *Because it's not about one of us; it's about all of us.*
When we gather, connect, and share, something happens. We change. We grow.
We want hearty exchanges with the people we love and safe places to fall.
We want to unpeel the layers and offer the best of ourselves.
Our best is rarely perfect, but that's OK.
We'll take real over perfect any day. And real happens here.

We have learned what it means to experience God's love in a real way
and renewed our belief in each other (and ourselves).

When we look at you, we see untapped power that can change the world.
Let's fan that flame and make things happen. We can do this. You are not alone.
We've readied a place for you to come in, to share, to heal, and to dance . . .

To BELONG.

JEN hatmaker   **ANGELA** davis   **NICHOLE** nordeman   **SHAUNA** niequist   **SHARON** irving   **PATSY** clairmont

At live events that bring women together in arenas across the country, remarkable
communicators gather with thousands of women to talk about how to live a fun,
faith-filled, purposeful life. There are plenty of personal stories, music, laughter, and
maybe even some tears in this Friday-night-to-Saturday event, where every woman
can find a place to belong.

**Get acquainted and find how you can be a part
of the BELONG community at BELONGtour.com.**

CP1103